Con

How Ukraine Survived: Inside the Strategy to Stop Russia's Invasion

William Spaniel

Cover image: President Joe Biden walks with Ukrainian President Volodymyr Zelensky at St. Michael's Cathedral. Official White House Photo by Adam Schultz.

About the Author

William Spaniel is an associate professor at the University of Pittsburgh who specializes in international security, bargaining, and nuclear proliferation. Prior to starting at Pitt, he received a PhD in political science from the University of Rochester and was a postdoctoral fellow at Stanford University. He is the creator of the popular YouTube channel and book series *Game Theory 101*. You can subscribe to his channel at: https://www.youtube.com/c/gametheory101.

Foreword

Writing about historical wars is difficult. Writing about ongoing wars is *more* difficult, especially when much of the focus is on the insider military and political strategy. This book attempts to make sense of what occurred during the first four phases of Russia's invasion of Ukraine: the initial attack, attrition in the spring and summer of 2022, Ukraine's Kharkiv and Kherson counteroffensives, and the following winter lull that transitioned into Ukraine's summer 2023 counteroffensive. I wrote it from August to November 2023. To my knowledge, everything in the book was accurate at the time of production.

However, this will not be the last word on the war. New facts may come to light as the war continues (or ends) that may cause us to reevaluate some earlier aspects of the conflict. I am careful to flag elements of the narrative that are unclear or speculative, but there are limits to doing this.

The Battle of Hostomel Airport

At 8 am, on February 24, 2022, a fleet of tanks, trucks, armored personnel carriers, and other vehicles departed from the southern tier of Belarus. About six hours earlier, Russian President Vladimir Putin had gone on national television to deliver an address. After enumerating a series of grievances against Ukraine, he announced the start of a "special military operation." Russia and Ukraine were now at war.

However, what that actually meant was unclear at the time. Russia had already been engaged in a protracted conflict with Ukraine for the previous eight years. It began with the very public annexation of Crimea, an autonomous peninsula in the southeast of Ukraine. Beyond having a high concentration of ethnic Russians, the Crimean city of Sevastopol harbored Russia's Black Sea Fleet. Having secured that goal openly, the interim eight years shifted the form of the conflict to a shadow war. Two separatist regions in Eastern Ukraine formed immediately after the fall of Crimea in the Donetsk and Luhansk oblasts. Few doubted that Russia underwrote the funding and provided troops in an unofficial capacity.

It did not take long to understand that the "special military operation" went far beyond the eastern border regions, though. The fleet departing from Belarus represented the main component of Russia's offensive against Kyiv, the Ukrainian capital. What followed on its tail would later become known as the Russian Kyiv Convoy. At its peak, it stretched 64 kilometers and seemed like an unstoppable juggernaut.

Although no one in Ukraine realized it yet, what was about to unfold in the relatively unassuming town of Hostomel would arguably become the single most important event in Ukrainian history. The stakes could not have been higher: the country itself was on the line. If

Ukraine failed, Russian soldiers would have established a critical foothold into the country's interior. The Kyiv Convoy would have obtained a vital connecting point, and hordes more soldiers and materiel would have flooded into Ukraine.

Ukraine's problems would have only grown from there. President Volodymyr Zelensky would have been captured—or worse. Ukraine would have become like a headless corpse. Not much after that, the rest of the country would have received the Crimea treatment, with Moscow formally annexing it into the Russian Federation bit by bit. Putin's dreams of becoming a modern-day Peter the Great could have finally been fulfilled. At that point, his legacy would have been forever cemented in the upper echelon of Russian leaders.

And the news would get even worse for Kyiv: the makeshift Ukrainian defense force was going to lose this battle. It was going to hurt—and hurt bad. The scene would look less like a war in the year 2022 and more like something out of a post-apocalyptic movie fit for Hollywood.

Yet somehow, someway, Ukraine would hold on.

The Target: Hostomel Airport

Founded in 1494, Hostomel was a small town of 18,000 people, located 26 kilometers northwest of Kyiv. Before the war, its main economic driver was Hostomel Airport, also known as Antonov Airport due to Antonov Airlines' enormous presence there. Despite its prominence in the local economy, to the average person, it was an unassuming facility built in 1959 meant for cargo runs.

By contrast, Boryspil International was Ukraine's largest airport. It sat 31 kilometers east of Kyiv and processed 15 million passengers yearly. Ukraine's second busiest airport outside of Crimea was Kyiv International, located just southeast of the city center. Those were the airports that everyone knew and flew into and out of, especially for international travel. Prior to 2022, outsiders may have regarded Hostomel as an irrelevant airstrip they might see as they flew into one of the other airports. It was not worth a second thought.

Nevertheless, Hostomel Airport had one claim to fame: it was the home of the Antonov Airlines An-225. It was the world's largest aircraft: 84 meters long and with an 88.4-meter wingspan. With those statistics, the An-225 was something that Ukrainians were very proud of. They made model toys of it. The plane would do fly-overs at patriotic parades. Never mind that it also could haul more cargo than any other plane in the world.

Oddly, the An-225's history was a microcosm for the events that were about to take place. It was originally a product of the Soviet era, first flown on December 21, 1988, specifically constructed to transport the Buran spaceplane. Buran was the Soviet answer to the American Space Shuttle program—in fact, when placed in a photo lineup with the Space Shuttle, it is easy to think that it *was* an American craft. However, the Buran had a slightly larger payload capacity and could return significantly more from orbit. That made the Buran incredibly large and heavy. To transport it around the Soviet Union, Moscow also needed an enormous plane. Hence the Soviet Union built the An-225.

But the plane's glory days were behind it. Through no fault of the An-225, the Buran system was a complete bust. Its only flight occurred on November 15, 1988—an unmanned three-and-a-half-hour trip. From a technical standpoint, the launch was a triumph. That did not stop the Soviet Union from collapsing, though. Russia did not have the money to continue the program, so Russia's first president Boris Yeltsin canceled it in 1993. The whole affair represented a Soviet failure and the inability of Kremlin leadership to establish a glorious legacy.

By November 2021, it appeared that Moscow was trying to take a different legacy-defining action. The Buran, the An-225, and Hostomel Airport were far from anyone's mind. Instead, the focus was on the border between Ukraine's borders—both with Russia and with Belarus, Russia's closest ally. At least 100,000 Russian soldiers had amassed there. The next three months were a jumbled mess of maneuvering, duplicity, and conflicting messaging. By January 2022, however, U.S. intelligence became convinced that an invasion was imminent. President Joe Biden dispatched William Burns, the director of the Central Intelligence Agency, to Kyiv on the 12th to discuss their findings.

Nevertheless, Ukraine publicly downplayed the threat of war. Zelensky was not naïve—he believed that U.S. intelligence could be right. Instead, it was a cold economic calculation. Ukrainian policymakers worried that the endless talk of war would drive all the economic investment out of Ukraine. If a war were to start afterward, Ukraine did not want to fight from a position as if it had been under *de facto* economic sanctions for months prior.

Moreover, there was some chance that it would all ultimately go nowhere. After all, Russia had undergone an earlier mobilization in March and April 2021. This did not culminate with an actual invasion, and the Russian troops partially withdrew by June. Perhaps the second mobilization was more of the same: Russia would rattle its saber but not pursue things any further. Because that was a plausible interpretation of what was happening, Ukraine had not yet gone into full defense mode. Its alert status was elevated, but a complete Ukrainian mobilization was not yet in the picture.

Ukraine's posture over at Hostomel Airport reflected this. Only 300 troops were stationed there at the time. Further, these were merely national guard troops—essentially armed caretakers. The true heavy hitters—and

Ukraine's heavy equipment—were over in Donetsk and Luhansk dealing with the separatists. Obviously, the Hostomel contingent seemed relatively understaffed. But Ukraine thought the odds that Russia would attack were acceptably low. Even the 300 troops stationed at Hostomel cracked jokes about how the United States' endless warnings were blowing the threat out of proportion.

They were wrong.

Russia's Hostomel Strategy

On the morning of February 24, 2022, the An-225 sat quietly at Hostomel Airport within its massive hangar. In the days earlier, managers at the airport were worried enough that they began moving their aircraft to safer locations. Unfortunately, the An-225 was at the back of the line. National prestige could not overcome basic mechanics. Following its most recent flight—a mission to ferry 90 tons of COVID tests from China to Denmark—the plane had to undergo routine maintenance before going airborne again. With just a few more hours of work, it would be ready to leave later that day.

However, it was not meant to be. Putin's "special military operation" announcement began at 4:30 am Ukrainian time. Hostomel Airport found itself under almost immediate attack. The An-225 could no longer safely depart.

One way to win a war—or a special military operation for that matter—is to decapitate the opposing leadership. That was easier said than done here. Russia was using Belarus as a staging ground to get closer to Ukraine. Even so, it was still a 154-kilometer drive from the southern tip of Belarus to Kyiv. Moscow's solution instead was to establish a forward operating base close to the capital.

But where? Kyiv International Airport seemed like a good starting point. However, it was in the middle of a large population center and would have been naturally better defended. Then there was the fact that Kyiv International Airport's runway was only 2300 meters long. Military aircraft tend to be heavier and also carry heavy things—like those tanks Russia desperately needed to invade Kyiv. Consequently, military planes require longer runways.

The answer to both of those problems was Hostomel Airport. The town was just beyond the edge of the outer defense perimeter that Ukraine would later establish for Kyiv. Ukraine would certainly try to defend it, but its location in a small town meant a slower response and that Russia would better observe where the counterattack was coming from. Meanwhile, its focus on cargo planes was also desirable. Like military aircraft, cargo planes tend to be heavy and thus need long runways. In that regard, the An-225 loved the 3500 meters Hostomel's strip had to offer.

More subtly, Hostomel's position to the northwest of Kyiv was vital. Boryspil also sat outside of Kyiv's main population center and had an even longer runway of 4000 meters. However, it was east and slightly south of Kyiv. The latter direction meant that Russia would have to overshoot the capital before establishing Boryspil as a forward operating base. The former direction conflicted with the Kyiv Convoy's plan to follow the western bank of the Dnipro River. This was Ukraine's main waterway and played a major role throughout the conflict across the country. It flowed south from Belarus, cut Kyiv in half, and then turned southeast before dipping due south once again. Finally, the Dnirpo shifted southwest at Zaporizhzhia and flowed into the Black Sea just past Kherson. For the current battle in question, the Dnipro's bisection of Kyiv meant that Russia had to choose which path to take or voluntarily split its army. Ultimately, Russia chose to bomb Boryspil rather than control it at the beginning of the war.

In any case, with the target narrowed down to Hostomel Airport, Russia's plan was simple. First, use a combined assault to capture the runway. Second, land everything the army needed to stage an attack on Kyiv. Then capture the capital. With that complete, sit back and watch the rest of Ukraine fall apart. With any luck, Moscow could have its troops back home by Easter.

It was easy, really—in theory, at least.

The First Shots

Early on, it seemed easy indeed. Three-and-a-half hours after Putin's announcement, or 8 am in Hostomel, a group of Mi-8 transport helicopters with hundreds of Russian troops departed from an airstrip near Myzar, Belarus. Ka-52 attack helicopters provided support, aiming to soften the target and allow for a safe deployment of the ground forces. They stayed low, trying to fly under Ukraine's radar, and followed the Dnipro River south. Once they hit the northern edge of Kyiv, the helicopters turned sharply west and aimed straight for Hostomel. Ukrainian missiles downed two of them at this point, but the group was still large enough to press on to the airport.

Once there, Ukraine tried to fight back. However, this was a new experience, especially for the reservists. The separatists in Donetsk and Luhansk had no air force. Rather, in the east, it was all about World War I style trench warfare. Ukrainian troops were simply not accustomed to fighting an opponent in the skies. To make matters worse, Russia knew where Ukraine's airport defense systems were located and struck them ahead of time. After the battle, Kyiv would blame a treasonous airport employee for relaying that information to Moscow. Despite that, Ukraine showed some ability to fight back by downing at least one more of the Ka-52s.

But it was no matter. Ukraine could only slow Russia's movements, not stop them. Three hours into the battle, the Mi-8 helicopters deployed their paratroopers and began the ground assault. Ukraine's 300 national guard soldiers were no match for a combined air and ground operation.

Running out of ammunition, Ukraine chose to retreat. Russia took control of the airport, surveying the scene and deciding how to best implement the next part of its plan.

If this were the end of the story, it might also have been the end of modern Ukraine. We may never know exactly what Russia planned to fly in, but the common belief is that eighteen Ilyushin Il-76 planes were headed from Pskov oblast in Russia and preparing to land at Hostomel. Since its first flight in 1971, the Il-76 became a workhorse for the Soviet military. Undoubtedly, the fleet of eighteen held countless Russian soldiers and weapons. Following a successful landing in Hostomel, they planned to set their sights on Kyiv, with a very high chance of success.

What Russia intended to do once there was ambiguous at the time. Hold the city hostage until Ukraine released its eastern regions to Russia? Yes, at a bare minimum. Do that and replace Zelensky with a puppet government? Possibly. Outright annex the entire country? That would have been hard to accomplish without facing a massive insurgency, but maybe. Whatever the answer was, observers feared that the loss of the airport was the first domino toward the end of Ukraine as we knew it.

Unless Ukraine had a secret…

Ukraine's Backup Plan

Flashback to January 12, 2022. With U.S. intelligence convinced Russia was about to invade, CIA Director Burns traveled to Kyiv. But he was not there just to discuss the gravity of the situation. He also came with something else: Russia's battleplans. And all signs pointed toward the same place: Hostomel Airport. After all, it was a logical first step. Only eight years prior, Russia had used Simferopol Airport as a similar air bridge during the annexation of Crimea.

Thus, though Ukraine only had 300 national guard soldiers actively defending the facility, there was a backup plan. That was bad news for the Russian troops in

Hostomel. They were in a precarious position. The mission began with helicopters inserting them deep behind enemy lines. Such an operation meant that they lacked the armored vehicles they would want to use to protect themselves over the long term. Rather, those would have to come in via the Kyiv Convoy.

Meanwhile, the Ukrainian armed forces were in relatively good shape at that point despite facing a much larger opponent. Russia dove headfirst into the war, initiating the ground invasion immediately after Putin's televised declaration. There was no period where Russia softened up Ukrainian targets with aerial bombings and cruise missile strikes. These were the hallmarks of the U.S. "shock and awe" military strategy used in contemporary invasions precisely because it made the infantry's job much easier.

Still capable of coordinating countermeasures and with the clock ticking due to the Il-76s, Ukraine had to make a play. Chief of the armed forces Valery Zaluzhny therefore sent in the cavalry. This included Ukrainian special forces, a mechanized brigade, a rapid reaction brigade, and the Georgian Legion. The latter was especially eager to enter the fray, as it was founded in 2014 by Georgians looking to settle the score with Russia after their war in 2008. Additional support came from Ukrainian artillery, which now pointed at the airport. Finally, the Ukrainian Air Force scrambled to counteract any Russian aircraft intending to harass Ukraine's ground forces.

The push began with paratroopers approaching the airport from the west. Almost immediately, they ran into problems. Like any self-respecting airport, Hostomel had walls that protected the facility from intruders. Ironically, those "intruders" were now Ukrainians. Russian gunfire pinned down those who made it over, and the walls prevented those on the outside from providing cover fire.

However, two more units arrived shortly thereafter, one from the north and the other from the southeast.

All told, the chaos on the ground prevented the Il-76s from landing. Even if they could avoid direct fire from the counterattacking Ukrainians, the runway was still a mess. Understanding that 300 reservists were unlikely to hold the airport on their own, Ukraine parked every spare vehicle they could find on the runway. One of the helicopters Ukraine shot down earlier in the fight landed on the runway as well, creating another obstacle. For any plane to land, Russian troops needed to first clear a path.

That was no small task in the middle of an ongoing battle. The theme for the day was chaos. According to the leader of the Georgian Legion, running short on ammo, they used cars to try to run down Russian soldiers. Two Ukrainian Su-24s dropped bombs along the runways. The combined efforts meant that the force ratio remained favorable to Ukraine over the short term.

Overwhelmed and lacking cover, Russian troops had no choice but to retreat to the woods around the airport. According to a Russian logbook recovered by the *New York Times*, up to 300 of the Russian paratroopers died in the battle. By the time February 24 ended, Ukraine was back in control of the airport.

Russia Resurgent

The next day, a Russian column coming from Belarus and going through Chernobyl reached Hostomel. This was the prelude of the Kyiv Convoy. And although the convoy would eventually become a punchline, this was still only 24 hours into the war. All of the convoy's logistical failures were not yet present. Consequently, the force ratio swung back into Russia's favor.

This time, Ukraine lacked an effective reply. With no better alternative, the Ukrainian troops retreated. Fighting spilled over to the remainder of the city and into the surrounding towns. Hostomel Airport changed hands once again, now back under Russian control. The airport would stay that way for the remainder of the first bit of the war.

However, "airport" might not be the right word. The direct engagements, Ukrainian air strikes, Ukrainian artillery, and whatever further sabotage operations Ukrainian soldiers may have engaged in overnight had rendered the runway unusable. Russia won the fight but failed to accomplish its main objective: to secure an immediate air bridge into Kyiv.

And the An-225? It again acts as a microcosm for the entire situation. Hangars are meant to protect planes from the elements, not small arms fire, explosions, and aerial bombardments. By the end of the battle, its 88.4-meter wingspan sat there in tatters. Sections of it looked like a guillotine had sliced right through the aircraft. But Ukrainians took inspiration from its sacrifice—fitting given that the An-225's nickname *Mriya* translates to inspiration.

Russian soldiers ignored the An-225's carcass and left it to rot in its hangar. Instead, once the installation was secured, they began clearing debris and repairing the runway. By March 7, Russia was using the airport effectively. But by that point, the main danger to Ukraine had passed. Ukraine may have lost the battle, but in doing so, it gave itself a chance to survive the war.

The Kremlin's Miscalculation

Had Russia quickly secured Hostomel Airport on February 24, 2022, and landed its troops, the trajectory of the war would have followed a very different path. As it stood, Russia's failure there revealed a number of deeper mistakes that would set the pace for the rest of the war. But to appreciate those problems, we must rewind to February 20.

On that date, somewhere deep inside the Kremlin, Putin made one of the most important decisions in post-Cold War history: he gave the final approval for Russia's invasion of Ukraine. This decision would not match the public drama that unfolded at Hostomel or the other battles to come. Nevertheless, it would frame everything else that would happen during the war. This has to be true on some level, of course, because without the decision to start an invasion, no invasion happens at all. But that is not the point. Rather, *how* Putin arrived at this decision would dictate Russia's strategy for the remainder of the conflict.

Unfortunately for Ukraine, the Kremlin was about to make a massive miscalculation that would cause great pain and suffering across the country. Fortunately for Ukraine, that miscalculation also left open a window for Ukraine to survive.

Building to the Invasion

For the three months prior to February 2022, Russia had been slowly shipping troops and materiel westward. Some of this rested along its traditional borders with Ukraine. Some lied in Russia-annexed Crimea, the peninsula that Ukraine lost eight years earlier. The rest was in Belarus, due north of Kyiv.

Worldwide, geopolitical tensions were on the rise. The recent rhetoric coming from Moscow had been nothing but hostile. Russia broadly objected to expansion of the North Atlantic Treaty Organization. Founded in 1949 by primarily Western European countries interested in deterring Soviet interference, the alliance had been slowly progressing eastward. Former Soviet Bloc countries began requesting membership, largely as a way to counterbalance Russia and its imperialist legacy. 2004 was a particularly embarrassing year for Moscow, when Estonia, Latvia, and Lithuania—three former republics of the Soviet Union—joined NATO. Almost two decades later, Russia worried that Ukraine would become the fourth.

However, when it came to Russian frustration with Ukraine, the NATO issue was perhaps the tip of the iceberg. From its birth in 1991, Ukraine straddled two worlds, east versus west. Political divisions within the country reflected this. The western half looked forward to integration with Western partners and membership in the European Union. Pockets of the east, many of its citizens primarily speaking Russian, sought to retain a close connection with Moscow. They may have overwhelmingly voted for independence at the end of the Cold War, but cultural ties to the east still ran strong.

In 2014, those tensions came to a head. Ukraine's president at the time, Viktor Yanukovych, shared the eastern half of his country's warm feelings for Russia. Nevertheless, his campaign in 2010 pledged to find common ground. As part of that, he supported a trade deal with the European Union, which many saw as a precursor to EU membership. At the last minute, though, he pulled support in favor of a similar deal with Russia.

The backlash in Ukraine was immediate. Protestors took to the streets. By February 2014, Yanukovych realized that he could not undo his mistake. He fled the country on the 21st, and a western-oriented government rose in his place. Russia took advantage of the political chaos in Kyiv to annex Crimea. Simultaneously, Moscow covertly built separatist movements in Luhansk and Donetsk, two Ukrainian oblasts on the border with Russia.

Tensions ebbed and flowed during the eight-year period in between. A ceasefire agreement known as Minsk I was signed in September 2014 but almost immediately failed. Its replacement, February 2015's Minsk II agreement, remained in place until the invasion. Nevertheless, the region was anything but peaceful, and casualties continued to trickle in. Even so, the 2022 Russian mobilization represented a new low. The United States, for one, was convinced that Russia would invade. Ukraine was desperately trying to downplay expectations that a full-scale war would begin.

And Russia? Well, officially, Moscow did not even acknowledge that any mobilization was happening. Instead, Russian troops were merely engaging in war games.

In reality, all of Putin's pieces were in place. And on February 20, 2022, he would tell his generals to begin final preparations for an attack. The die was cast. The invasion would begin four days later.

What Putin did not yet realize was that his main intelligence organizations had collectively dropped the ball. Within weeks—notwithstanding the failures at Hostomel—it would become clear that he had made a major mistake. Russia would not turn the war into a cakewalk. And if Russia finishes the war with any material gains at all, the substantial costs of fighting will offset any of those benefits.

The deeper question is why. Why did Vladimir Putin, a former KGB foreign intelligence officer who before 2022 was well-regarded for his political shrewdness, make such a colossal error?

Putin's Rise to Power

In the aftermath of the invasion, it became fashionable to blame the situation on some fundamental part of Russian culture or deficits in Vladimir Putin's strategic calculus. However, the story of the historic miscalculation is actually about Russia's institutional core rotting and the country's democratic backsliding.

The saga began on December 31, 1999. While the rest of the world was preparing to celebrate the turn of the millennium, Putin was about to get his big break. After leaving the KGB, Putin worked as an advisor to the mayor of Leningrad, which would quickly return to the Saint Petersburg monicker. That led to a position in Moscow, and then a position as deputy chief of President Boris Yeltsin's staff. That turned into director of the Federal Security Service, or FSB, which was the KGB's successor aimed toward former Soviet states. By the end of 1999, Putin received a promotion to prime minister, and thus was first in the line of succession to the presidency. That became relevant on New Year's Eve, when Yeltsin, facing declining health and possibly worse polling numbers, chose to resign.

Putin became acting president. Per constitutional rules, an election occurred three months later to decide on a full-fledged president. The field was crowded, but the outcome was not close. Putin beat his nearest opponent, Gennady Zyuganov of the Communist Party, by almost 24% of the vote. Acting President Putin became just regular President Putin.

Western leaders were cautiously optimistic at the time. The Yeltsin years had left a mark—they also began with a similar optimism, but that had faded over the years. However, after becoming U.S. president in 2001, George W. Bush believed that Putin would finally be a Russian leader that the West could work with. Their initial meetings were cordial, and Putin was the first world leader to call Bush following the September 11 terrorist attacks.

Back in Russia, things were also going well for Putin. His first standard election was on the calendar for 2004, and reelection was no problem. Once again faced with an opponent from the Communist Party, Putin earned 71.9% of the vote to only 13.8% for Nikolay Kharitonov. That guaranteed Putin's presidency would continue until May of 2008.

Nevertheless, the 2008 Russian presidential election presented a problem. Per the constitution as it existed, presidents could not serve more than two terms consecutively. It was, in theory, time for Putin to walk away.

But the constitution was not a real problem. Behind the scenes, Putin was eliminating any sort of institutions that restricted his influence. By some accounts, this began even before Putin became acting president. In September 1999, a wave of apartment bombings swept over Russia. Putin, at the time still prime minister, took charge of the crisis response. The official Russian account states that Chechen terrorists perpetrated the attacks. However, skeptics believe that Putin was behind them—or at least Russian entities sympathetic to him were responsible. If so, the endgame was to raise Putin's domestic profile, create a rally-'round-the-flag effect, and facilitate a transition of power.

Regardless of the true nature of the September 1999 apartment bombings, Putin wasted little time consolidating power once in office. On the more public front, this meant capturing the Russian media. Virtually everything became state-run, turned pro-Putin, or was taken off the air. Freedom of the press was no more. Internally, it meant stripping any potential challengers from power and ensuring that Putin's United Russia party had no peer competitors. The Soviet Union and communism were long gone, but autocracy was returning to the motherland.

Without any true challengers but still wanting to keep up outward appearances, Putin willingly left the office of the president in 2008, consistent with his constitutional obligations. Dmitry Medvedev, previously Putin's chief of staff and later his first deputy prime minister, became president.

Putin could have taken this moment to quietly retreat to a dacha and spend the rest of his days fishing along local waterways. He was popular among Russian citizens. Yes, Putin's control over the media distorted that popularity to some degree, but a large portion of it was authentic. Whereas the Yeltsin years became associated with economic catastrophe, Putin had converted Russia's latent power to something tangible. The days of the Soviet empire may have passed, but he could have retired as a Russian founding father.

Instead, Putin sidled into the prime minister's position. On paper, Medvedev was in charge. In practice, it was Putin all along.

Furthermore, the constitution only proscribed three *consecutive* terms. It did not say anything about three nonconsecutive terms. Putin's move to prime minister was just to bide time. When the next election came in 2012, Putin ran again. He won without issue, and Medvedev swapped to prime minister.

In the meantime, Putin pushed forward reforms to the constitution. Presidential terms expanded to six years. And given all of the control Putin was exerting, he unsurprisingly won a fourth term overall in 2018. But the same institutions—or lack of institutions—that had kept Putin in power for more than 22 years were about to cause Russia's undoing.

Russian Intelligence and Ukraine's Response

Soon after he won the 2018 election, Putin set his sights on extending Russia's reach into Ukraine. Part of this was to push back against NATO's movement into Eastern Europe. Part of this was to specifically stop the post-Maidan Revolution shift in Ukrainian politics away from Russia and toward the European Union and NATO. Part of this was to finish the job after Russia annexed Crimea in 2014. And some of this was possibly pure ego, with Putin wishing to feed his desire for historical comparisons to Peter the Great, who had expanded imperial Russian borders during his 1682-1725 reign.

At the time, Putin began examining the plausibility of using a war to accomplish those goals. A successful operation hinged on two questions. First, would average Ukrainians resist Russian soldiers or treat them as liberators? And second, how would the West—and the international community more generally—respond to a Russian invasion?

Answering those questions, as will become clear in a moment, was easier in theory than in practice. Russian intelligence organizations formed a complicated web. Indeed, the potential for duplicate effort and generally inefficient allocation of intelligence assets perhaps foreshadowed the miscalculation to come. Outside analysis can only speculate on the precise details of how this worked, but what follows is an attempt to infer what happened.

At a minimum, Putin needed to consult the FSB, the intelligence agency he previously directed. Recall that it is the organization responsible for intelligence matters within the former Soviet Union. (The fact that Russia treats such countries as distinct from the rest of the world hints at the Kremlin's mindset.) All observable features indicated that the invasion of Ukraine would not be as simple as the Crimean cakewalk from 2014. No other Ukrainian region had Crimea's history of autonomy. Even the 1991 independence votes in Luhansk and Donetsk overwhelmingly supported freedom from Moscow.

Nevertheless, there was hope in Russia that Ukrainian regional fractionalization would help. The 2004 presidential election ended in controversy, a rerun of the final ballot, and pro-West candidate Viktor Yushchenko eventually beating Viktor Yanukovych. The 2010 election—the one that Yanukovych won—again showed clear East-West divisions within the country. The 2014 special election saw business magnate Petro Poroshenko win with pluralities in most oblasts but came in the shadow of civil unrest. In 2019, Volodymyr Zelensky also won broad geographic support, but there was still some level of regional fractionalization.

On the surface, Zelensky's ascension appeared to represent a compromise. He grew up in Eastern Ukraine, spoke Russian as his native language, and spent substantial time touring Russia as a part of his comedy career. However, by 2022, Zelensky's political popularity as president had plummeted. Russian intelligence believed, at a minimum, that invading troops could have played the role of savior within Eastern Ukraine, and perhaps that narrative could have gone further.

Had that been true, Russia's life would have been substantially easier as it fought to secure its most basic war aims in the east. This was a legacy of Russia's prior power play. The 2014 annexation of Crimea took advantage of the political chaos in Kyiv. Russia exploited the window of opportunity while it was open, knowing that it would need to sort out the negative consequences afterward. And, indeed, these negative consequences snowballed in the meantime.

One such problem was water. A sizeable chunk of Crimea's economy was based on agriculture. However, the peninsula's natural rainfall could not sustain its farmland. Instead, Crimea relied on the North Crimean Canal. Completed in 1975, the canal fed water from the Dnipro River through a dam in the city of Kakhovka, within Kherson Oblast. It then swept south through the rest of Kherson, supplying water to aqueducts along the way, before finally arriving in Crimea. Following Russia's annexation, Kyiv ordered the obvious countermeasure: it dammed the canal near the line of control. This was the best of both worlds for Ukraine. It halted the flow of water into the peninsula while still continuing the flow to Ukrainian farmers north of the dam.

The canal incident highlights a broader problem that Russia faced heading into the war. With Ukraine blocking travel to and from Crimea, the peninsula was effectively an island for Russia. Moscow partially rectified the problem in 2018 by building the Crimean Bridge, connecting the scantly populated Russian locality Taman to the Crimean city of Kerch. Still, it asked a great deal for a single bridge to serve as a lifeline for almost 2.5 million people on the peninsula.

As such, Russia sought a land bridge as a solution. This entailed traveling west from Rostov-on-Don, Russia's eleventh most populous city. Hugging the Sea of Azov, Russia could conquer the southern portion of Donetsk Oblast, Zaporizhzhia Oblast, and Kherson Oblast, before finally linking up with Crimea. Had Russian intelligence been correct, a sizable portion of Ukrainians in those areas would have switched loyalties. Another portion would have not cared enough to resist. Either way, Russia did not anticipate a drawn-out fight over the land bridge.

There were further hopes within Russian intelligence that a western offensive could have also yielded clean results. Russia seemed to have willing collaborators working on its payroll throughout the country. Their assignments ranged from giving Russian military planners a list of targets, to serving as a basis to form a post-war government, to giving away vital information about Ukrainian defenses. The issue became so acute that Zelensky later fired the head of Ukraine's internal security service in July 2022. The Kremlin wondered whether Ukrainian apathy extended further westward and beyond the Russian-speaking portions of the country.

Failing that, Russian intelligence speculated that a little chaos within the capital had the potential to go a long way. Russia had hoped that Zelensky himself would be a source of weakness. After all, Zelensky was an actor turned politician, famous for his anti-corruption stances and not his foreign policy credentials. Calculating his poor odds, he might have responded to an invasion by fleeing to a Western country and beginning a government in exile.

More broadly, Russia's dream was that the invasion of Ukraine would look something like the 2003 Iraq War. There, major combat operations only lasted a few weeks. Iraqi soldiers were quick to desert. It was a sensible choice—many did not view Saddam Hussein as a leader who was worth defending. Even those that did like Saddam could anticipate others deserting and calculate that their own resistance would be futile at that point. That left just the extreme Saddam loyalists for the U.S.-led coalition to mop up, which did not take much time.

All Russia apparently needed to worry about was a long, drawn-out insurgency. Indeed, the United States was resigned to this apparent inevitability. Intelligence officials in Washington abandoned hope regarding a traditional war, focusing last-minute training to Ukrainians on how to maximize an insurgency's effectiveness. But even if such an outcome came to fruition, it would not be the end of the world for Putin. Russia remained an autocracy, and Putin retained a vice grip on Russian media. A slow trickle of casualties is easy to hide under those circumstances, unlike the U.S. experience in Afghanistan and Iraq.

Moreover, Moscow had demonstrated its ability to weather long insurgencies before. The Soviet Union spent almost all of the 1980s combating such a challenge to Afghanistan's communist government before finally departing. And although that turned out to be politically untenable in the long run, Ukraine was different. It was part of Russia's "near abroad" and was under Moscow's direct control up until 1991. Russian citizens heralded the return of Crimea in 2014 as a major foreign policy accomplishment. Surely, their feelings regarding Kyiv would be more similar to Crimea than Kabul.

Russian Intelligence and the West's Response

The second question was how the West would react if Ukraine came under attack. This time, the primary intelligence service tasked with answering it is less clear. As mentioned earlier, the FSB was responsible for dealing with former Soviet countries, like Ukraine. The Foreign Intelligence Service, or SVR, was responsible for intelligence on remaining countries. This particular question straddled the line, with the topic of how SVR-domain countries felt about FSB-domain countries.

But regardless of who was in charge, it was well-known in Moscow that the United States and its partners supported Ukraine in broad strokes. They were happy with the 2014 Maidan Revolution that sent Viktor Yanukovych scrambling to Russia—so much so that the Russian narrative of these events is that of a CIA-initiated coup. Long-term integration of Ukraine into the European Union and NATO were also in the cards.

However, Moscow was skeptical about just how much the United States and Western Europe were willing to pay in support of the Ukrainian cause. And if the West did not care much, certainly China, India, and the rest of the world would not either.

Much of this skepticism stemmed from the 2014 annexation of Crimea. This was a major turn of events. Since World War II, there has been a strong international norm against unilateral changes in territory. It is even enshrined in Article 2, Section 4 of the United Nations Charter, which instructs member states to "refrain…from the threat or use of force against the territorial integrity of any state." More relevant to the specific discussion at hand, Russia had signed the Budapest Memorandum in 1994. By doing so, Moscow promised to uphold the existing border in exchange for Ukraine signing the Nuclear Non-Proliferation Treaty.

In sum, Crimea was the largest violation of territorial integrity in recent memory. And the West's response? A lot of verbal criticism, but not a lot of hard ramifications. There was the standard economic sanctions package one would expect under these circumstances. They were "smart" sanctions in the sense that they targeted specific people in Russia—those that might have policy influence with Putin. They were not generalized sanctions that would devastate the Russian economy or force its military industry to collapse. Nothing approached how the United States responded to Iraq's invasion of Kuwait in 1990 or what the Western response in February 2022 would ultimately look like.

Within the global institutional settings, not much happened either. Western countries all but monopolized the Group of Eight, a political forum for the world's most advanced economies. Consequently, they simply kicked out Russia and returned to being the Group of Seven, as they were at the end of the Cold War. The United Nations General Assembly also passed Resolution 68/262 on the territorial integrity of Ukraine. It condemned the Russian annexation, though substantial portions of Asia, Africa, and South America either voted against it or abstained. Regardless, for United Nations resolutions to have meaningful impact, they must go through the Security Council. A similar declaration never made it through there. As a future chapter will delve deeper into, this was because Russia had veto power and could simply exercise it. All told, Russia hardly blinked at its punishment.

Furthermore, the time between 2014 and 2022 only indicated weaker resolve from the West. Arms transfers to Ukraine remained a critical policy question in the intervening years. Though Crimea fell without a fight, Ukraine did not simply let the Russian-sponsored separatist movements in Luhansk and Donetsk declare independence. Rather, the period in between featured the War in Donbas, named after the broader region that Luhansk and Donetsk occupy. And while any transfers made before 2022 were intended to aid Ukraine in Donbas, they retrospectively would have been helpful against a general invasion.

In any case, the arms were not forthcoming to the extent Ukraine desired. The Obama administration was only willing to provide training, not lethal aid. Plans for arms transfers had to wait for the Trump administration. The most notable of these were a sale of javelin missiles, which can independently home in on the weak points of Russian tanks. However, the continued execution of transfers became politically polarized. The peak of this problem manifested itself during Trump's first impeachment scandal. On July 25, 2019, President Trump had a thirty-minute phone call with Zelensky. The call began as a congratulatory message, as Zelensky's party had just won parliamentary elections. But the real issue of the day was that Trump had frozen Ukrainian military aid earlier that month.

After the pleasantries, the conversation shifted to Hunter Biden. Hunter is the son of Joe Biden, who had announced his candidacy for the 2020 presidential election three months earlier. During the Obama administration, Hunter Biden held a position on the board of Burisma, a large holding company for Ukrainian oil and gas. Given Joe Biden's position as vice president at the time—never mind Ukraine's legacy of corruption—many within the administration worried that his hiring created the appearance of a conflict of interest. And, indeed, it seemed that Hunter Biden had no direct expertise to confer onto Burisma. To make matters worse, Obama had tasked Joe Biden with helping Ukraine make reforms and prosecute corrupt individuals. Trump believed Hunter's connection went further, and years later he was in a position to press the subject. On the call, he told Zelensky that "[t]here's a lot of talk about Biden's son, that Biden stopped the prosecution, and a lot of people want to find out about that so whatever you can do with the Attorney General [William Barr] would be great."

The phone call turned into a scandal after a whistleblower came forward in September 2019. Congressional Democrats saw this as a *quid-pro-quo*: that Trump withheld Ukrainian aid but was willing to release it should Zelensky find political dirt on a potential 2020 presidential opponent. On December 18, the House of Representatives formally voted to impeach Trump. The vote regarding abuse of power passed 230 to 197, mostly along party lines. No Republicans voted yea, and only two Democrats voted nay. However, the Senate voted to acquit Trump on February 5, 2020. The vote on abuse of power failed 48-52, again mostly along party lines. This time, only Utah Senator Mitt Romney, the Republican Party's last presidential nominee before Trump, voted against his party's position.

No matter how Americans felt about Trump's culpability in the scandal, reality set in for everyone: aid to Ukraine was now a political issue. Moreover, it was the type of political issue that Putin sought to exploit.

Outside of the United States, Russia was also optimistic about how Europe might react. Before things turned sour, Germany worked with Russia to open the Nord Stream 1 pipeline in October 2011. It connected Russian gas fields near the Gulf of Finland and Saint Petersburg to hungry German markets. Its immediate success led to planning of the Nord Stream 2 pipeline to further increase flows. However, Berlin shared Washington's discomfort with Russia's annexation of Crimea. Nord Stream 1 continued operations but at a lower capacity. This obviated the need for Nord Stream 2, thereby pausing construction plans.

By 2018, though, the pipe laying was full steam ahead. Germany appeared ready to forgive and forget—or at least just forgive—and work toward the completion of the Nord Stream 2 pipeline, albeit with less enthusiasm. Gerhard Schroeder, Angela Merkel's predecessor as chancellor, continued to serve on the board of the Nord Stream's joint stock company. Completing the second pipeline would double German access to cheap Russian gas and create an industrial windfall. Many were critical of the policy, Trump among the most vocal. The harshest critiques compared it to the Molotov-Ribbentrop Pact, the agreement between Nazi Germany and the Soviet Union that divided Poland prior to World War II. Merkel, in particular, became publicly skeptical about U.S. sanctions that interfered with German energy policy. Allegations flew that the true U.S. gripe stemmed from Germany not installing liquid natural gas terminals, which would open the market to U.S. exports. All of these arguments would resurface months later in the war, but that is a topic for a later chapter.

Overall, the West's response to previous Russian incursions was disjointed and distant to say the least. From Russia's perspective, this was a sign that the West could not agree whether Ukraine was worth standing firm on. Given that, Russian intelligence hoped to get by with little more than a stronger slap on the wrist. In an optimistic scenario, an invasion could sow further discord into the NATO alliance, fracturing its otherwise uninterrupted progress since the end of the Cold War.

The Military's Confirmation

Putin was not receiving any better advice from his generals. On paper, the matchup between Russia and Ukraine was not much of a fight. The observable aspects tell a convincing story—with the caveat that obtaining clear data on military capabilities, especially as an outside analyst, is difficult. Still, the quantifiable metrics all showed Russian dominance. On gross domestic product, Russia led $1.8 trillion to $200 billion. On active military personnel, again Russia, by 1,000,000 to 209,000. Reserves also favored Russia, this time 2,000,000 to 900,000. On annual military spending, Russia beat Ukraine by an order of magnitude,

$62 billion to just $6 billion. That bought Russia 3400 tanks to Ukraine's 100, and 1400 combat aircraft versus 100.

Some of these discrepancies are overstated a bit. Russia's military spending also covers some amount of domestic security that had no bearing on the invasion. It includes Russia's nuclear weapons arsenal as well, which one *hopes* had no bearing on the invasion either even if the arsenal came up occasionally in Russian saber-rattling. Meanwhile, Ukraine only had one true geopolitical rival: Russia. Of course, Belarus functioned as an extension of Russian policy. But regardless, all of Ukraine's forces and materiel had a singular goal, and all were pointed in the corresponding direction.

In contrast, Moscow had more of a juggling act to perform. Deploying all Russian capabilities to the Ukrainian border was unacceptable. Kremlin planners worried that rival states might take advantage of the situation if Russia were laser-focused on Kyiv. And the rivals Russia had made were numerous. There was Finland, dating back to the 1939 Winter War and before. The 2008 summer war left Georgia with unfinished business. The Baltic states had a messy breakup from the Soviet Union. Lastly, of course, the United States and NATO more broadly were the top public enemy. If things went really haywire, even China and Japan could enter the picture.

Kremlin officials were also proud of the powerful, modern military they thought they had constructed. For a long time, corruption and morale problems within the Russian military were open secrets. In 2007, Putin appointed Anatoly Serdyukov to minister of defense, asking him to fix the system. Serdyukov's background hints at the fundamental problem the military had. He came from the Federal Tax Service, not the military, earning him the nickname "The Tax Man." Putin needed Serdyukov to use his bureaucratic prowess to fix the Russian system.

Only a little more than a year later, Serdyukov's job became further complicated. By all accounts, Russia won its 2008 war with Georgia. However, despite securing autonomy for the separatist regions of Abkhazia and South Ossetia, Russia's post-war analysis indicated that its military had *underperformed*. At the manpower level, poor coordination among Russian soldiers complicated otherwise straightforward missions. At the materiel level, poor maintenance procedures became apparent, with a substantial portion of equipment failing to ever cross the border.

Early indications suggested that the reforms had the intended effect. In September 2015, after years of giving political and military aid, Russia directly intervened in the Syrian Civil War. Many observers wondered whether this would be a repeat of 2008, where Russian forces would be effective but still underperform. Instead, Russian equipment appeared ready and well-maintained.

Six years later, the Biden administration wondered whether the experiences of 2008 or 2015 reflected the true Russia. To answer that, Biden dispatched William Burns to Moscow in November 2021. Burns was the director of the CIA but previously served as the U.S. ambassador to Russia. In other words, he had the perfect profile to ascertain Russian intentions as the buildup along the Belarusian border was in progress. His conversations with Kremlin officials quickly turned toward pride in Russia's renovated military, allegedly now free from the Soviet legacy that tainted its birth.

Interstate communication like this should always be taken with a grain of salt. The incentive to exaggerate one's own coercive capability is high. In this case, if other states were to take Moscow at its word, then they may take a more cautious approach in their relations with Russia. But then, if Russia never actually fixed its military, policymakers in Moscow could make the same declarations and gain the same benefits. Consequently, opposing countries have a difficult time differentiating between fact and fiction based purely on the words they hear from rivals.

Nevertheless, at least in this case, Burns' assessment was that Kremlin officials believed what they were saying. Russia would not see the errors of yesteryear recur in Ukraine.

But perhaps the most compelling source of the Kremlin's confidence was what had been happening over the prior eight years in Ukraine's outer edges. The annexation of Crimea was a clean operation that made Putin seem like a geopolitical mastermind. Unmarked Russian troops—called "little green men" because of the color of their uniforms and lack of insignia—simply entered the peninsula. Once there, they took possession of key control points and convinced Ukrainian resistance to either retreat north or switch loyalties. About half chose the latter option. Even if Kyiv had not been distracted with its own turmoil, it is not obvious what a calculated response from the central government could have done to stop Russia.

Back in 2022, the Kremlin knew that a complete replication of the Crimean operation across all of Ukraine was not possible. The sentiments that citizens of Kyiv had for Russia were not identical to the sentiments that Crimeans had. Returns from the 2004 and 2010 Ukrainian presidential elections demonstrated that. But Russia did not need that level of complicity to have success. At a minimum, Moscow expected an easier pathway through the eastern portions of Ukraine—those that more heavily favored Yanukovych and had more ethno-linguistic ties to Russia. That would leave more resources available to attack the capital. And if some within Kyiv also gave up, then it could have a cascading effect. Unlike Crimea, Russia would incur significant casualties. But those losses would be a small price to pay to expand the Kremlin's reach.

The interim years had given Russia some further evidence that this might work. In 2014, Russia executed another operation, this time in the eastern Donbas region of Ukraine. Recall that two nascent separatist movements with little hope of succeeding on their own sprung up in the Luhansk and Donetsk oblasts. Officially, Russia did not sponsor them. However, few doubt that Putin was unofficially signing orders to send more little green men to the regions. This external support was pivotal to preventing Ukraine's "Anti-Terrorist Operation" from regaining control of the breakaway regions.

By 2022, this War in Donbas had reached a stalemate, with trenches fit for World War I dug in on both sides. Oddly, this seemed like a positive sign for Moscow. Ukraine had racked up casualties over the years, allowing the separatist capitals to stay afloat. Furthermore, Russia had accomplished this while handicapping itself. As mentioned in the previous chapter, without official support from Moscow, the separatists ran no air operations in the Donbas. If Putin gave the go-ahead for a full invasion, rapid advances seemed likely. The greater show of force might have given Ukrainian citizens on the edge the motivation to cancel any further resistance.

Meanwhile, there was cause for optimism regarding Russia's push for Kyiv. Collaborators were on Russia's payroll even in Ukraine's western regions. That gave planners access to intelligence about Ukrainian air defenses. The scheme called for a rapid hit to them, which would allow Russia to obtain complete dominance over the skies. Fighter jets and bombers would then give ground troops a clear path into the capital. Timetables given to the invading soldiers had the expectation that they would arrive between 3 pm and midnight on the first day.

Russia was not alone with this optimistic assessment. U.S. intelligence was spot-on in publicizing Russia's intention to invade and shared the belief that Ukraine would lose rapidly. This assessment remained unchanged two days before the invasion began. With Moscow's mobilization looming, Ukraine's Minister of Foreign Affairs Dmytro Kuleba toured Washington, D.C., searching for some final support. One meeting on his agenda was with Chairman of the Joint Chiefs of Staff Mark Milley and Secretary of Defense Lloyd Austin. The conversation focused on how Ukraine could build an insurgency, not fight a conventional war.

Of course, there is an alternate universe where Russia's expectations would have been at least somewhat vindicated. Russia was just one airport battle away from making the war much easier for its invading forces. However, as we know from the last chapter, that effort failed. Instead, Putin was about to be hit with a cold dose of reality.

Pravda

Long ago, the Communist Party of the Soviet Union's official newspaper was titled *Pravda*. One translation for the word is "truth"; the irony of the name was not lost on anyone back then. Fast forward to 2022, and the news Putin was receiving from his intelligence officials was still far from being *pravda*.

Regarding the West, it was true that NATO countries were tepid in their response to the invasion of Crimea. But a land war in Europe? That was a true redline. The apparent dissension within NATO at the end of 2021 was not about willingness to support Ukraine, as Russian intelligence surmised. Rather, it stemmed from a difference in opinions from the various Western intelligence agencies about whether Putin was serious about the invasion.

Regarding Ukrainian resolve, Russian intelligence completely misread the situation. Zelensky was willing to fight. The Ukrainian people were willing and ready to rally around the flag. There would be no repeat of Crimea.

Ironically, Putin's own dominance over Russian institutions caused the problems ahead. Undoubtedly, some within the FSB and other intelligence arms were skeptical of the official reports. The issue for Putin was that his autocratic system had created sycophants. When officials are rewarded for following a leader's preferred policy regardless of the facts on the ground, intelligence as a whole begins to break down. Advisors start playing a guessing game of what the leader wants to hear rather than transmit information about the truth. Worse, those advisors have no incentive to put in the hours to learn what the actual good advice would be. After all, if they are never going to tell the leader bad news, why try to learn the *pravda*?

To be clear, the situation in Russia was not as bad as in true totalitarian states. For example, Saddam Hussein was known for murdering contrarian advisors, sometimes before the people in question could leave the building. In contrast, Russia still maintained a handful of functioning institutions. But even then, dissenters in Russia sometimes had trouble walking down a flight of stairs or not falling out of windows—or, much later in the war, keeping their planes in the sky.

Creating this incentive structure may seem crazy from a leader's perspective, as it will eventually cause the country to make major policy mistakes. Nevertheless, a leader's desire to repress potential challengers can take precedence. Moscow is especially familiar with this, going back to the days of the czar or the Soviet era. Speaking out against the leader's preferred policy will draw scrutiny, as it marks the advisor as a potential challenger.

The problem still arises even if the advisor has no inherent interest in mounting a challenge. Just being on the record as having a dissenting opinion can cause issues down the line. For example, suppose that the leader pursues what everyone ultimately learns is a terrible idea—say, initiating a difficult invasion that was supposed to be easy. As time passes, the public may become angry and demand changes at the top. Now whichever advisor was the contrarian becomes an obvious replacement candidate. As a result, any of those contrarian viewpoints from the FSB or other intelligence organizations were unlikely to reach the surface.

Meanwhile, the Russian military had not provided better guidance either. However, the problem there was less about drawing the wrong inference—those within the system knew the truth. Instead, the problem was more about systemic rot and lack of incentives to report that rot.

Soldiers in every country have a temptation to be lazy, whether they be Russian, Ukrainian, Western, or otherwise. After all, if your contribution is minimal and no one is going to notice you slacking off, why bother putting in the effort at all? This attitude permeated the Russian military from top to bottom. It was easier to just go along with the system rather than disrupt the corrupt harmony.

In fact, the Russian language has a specific word to capture this: *vranyo*. Alexandre might lie to Ivan about his war preparations. Ivan might know that Alexandre is lying to him. Further, Alexandre might know that Ivan knows that he is lying. Yet everyone pretends that this is normal. To object would raise the question of what should be done to fix the problem, and no one wants to go down that road.

What separated Russia from other countries and allowed *vranyo* culture to persist were Russian institutions—or lack thereof. Imagine that the U.S. army was a giant paper tiger, with nothing actually working despite billions of dollars spent. Just about everyone is to blame—from top to bottom, there is a rotten culture of laziness. This would make for a juicy scoop for all major news organizations, and its revelation would dominate the headlines for weeks. All it would take is a handful of patriotic soldiers who care about the U.S. military's weakness to blow the whistle. If doing so would lead to reforms, many would be willing to come forward.

Western militaries are not immune to scandals and boondoggles, but they are comparatively rare. The reason is that everyone along the chain of command—from generals up top to privates at the bottom—is aware of the media's oversight role. When waste and laziness cause problems, soldiers tend to make internal reports. Command then tends to confront the problems. The possibility that problems might boil over into the public sphere incentivizes militaries to investigate problems on their own and correct them.

In theory, autocratic governments could use media in a similar oversight role. The issue is that an unregulated media can turn critical of the government—and this is what truly terrifies autocracies. Oppressive governments rarely have enough security forces to quell a coordinated popular uprising against them. From a citizen's perspective, the problem is that arriving on a street corner to protest by oneself is a ticket to jail—or worse. The fear this instills keeps most citizens at home and allows autocratic governments to stay in power. However, by controlling the airwaves, the media can coordinate protests. As such, autocratic governments want to dominate the media to prevent that from happening.

Russia was no exception here. Long before the mobilization, Putin decided to fall toward the anti-media side of things. Two of Russia's largest news agencies, TASS and RIA Novosti, are state owned and have roots from the Soviet era. In 2007, an agency called Roskomnadzor formed to act as an oversight board for mass media. This allowed the federal government to exert influence over *all* outlets, state-owned or otherwise. By 2021, these and other measures plunged Russia to 150 out of 180 countries in the Press Freedom Index.

But come February 2022, Putin was about to experience the downside of media capture.

Ukraine Casts Doubt

Perhaps the greatest irony of the invasion is that Putin was not privy to what Ukraine knew about *his own* military. During the leadup to the war, rumors circulated in Ukraine that the Russian military was in trouble. This went beyond mere problems with basic corruption—the speculation was that *vranyo* culture had consumed every bit of the institution.

The possibility of endemic corruption was an open secret. Ukraine was fully aware of how Putin appointed Anatoly Serdyukov to fix the problem in 2007. But whether those reforms were successful was unclear. As if to create a microcosm of Russia's greater problems, Putin dismissed Serdyukov in 2012 under suspicions of corruption. Serdyukov was married to the daughter of Viktor Zubkov, a Russian prime minister under Putin. Sometime between 2010 and 2012, Serdyukov began an affair with an employee at the Ministry of Defense. On October 25, 2012, authorities conducted a search of the mistress's apartment. Inside were more than a million dollars of assets *and* Serdyukov. Whether she was acting as a conduit for illicit payments to Serdyukov is unclear. Regardless, the son-in-law of a powerful Putin ally was caught in an affair. Putin dismissed him a couple of weeks later.

This was one of many attempts to clean up Russian military corruption. But as the end of that story indicates, the success of any of them was ambiguous. Even Serdyukov's successor as minister of defense, Sergei Shoigu, was subject to many questions about his net worth and how he acquired it. As such, policymakers in Kyiv needed to get a better idea of the situation before crafting a response to Putin's potential invasion. They called upon the Ukrainian Foreign Intelligence Service, known as the SZRU, to investigate the situation further.

In the weeks prior to the invasion, the SZRU dispatched agents into Russia to infiltrate military installations. One team reported having observed tank, after tank, after tank lining up for *something*, which we know in retrospect was the invasion. However, the support infrastructure was missing. The mechanics necessary to service those tanks were nowhere in sight. Instead, the tanks were just sitting there, left to rust.

Worse for Russia, the soldiers that Ukrainian intelligence could locate did not show much interest in preparing for combat. Instead, they were trying to sell anything they could—Russian military property or otherwise—so they could buy more alcohol. Russia's public portrayal of its military—with shiny armored vehicles and smiling soldiers parading down Red Square during every May 9 Victory Day Parade—did not align at all with what Ukrainian intelligence observed.

The implied problems for Russian military planners went further down the system. It is one thing for each Russian soldier along the chain of command to skim a few rubles from a military contract. At least that type of corruption is efficient. Policymakers can plan for it, realize they will lose a few thousand rubles, and simply add it to the budget. The money the government loses equals the money that the soldiers pocket.

However, what Ukrainian intelligence witnessed was a much deeper inefficiency that Russian corruption had created. If a soldier strips a tank of its valuable metals and petrol, the sale price on the black market might give him a tidy sum for a day's work. Nevertheless, the remaining carcass of the tank represents millions of rubles wasted. In sum, the soldier makes a modest gain, and the military suffers a gigantic loss. Unlike skimming money, the government cannot adequately compensate for this in the budget. It just makes military ventures impossible.

The solution, of course, is oversight—specifically, the type of oversight that Russia's autocratic institutions had rendered ineffective years earlier.

Putin Pulls the Trigger

It is hard to believe Putin was oblivious to what was happening around him. *Vranyo* culture is a legacy of the

Soviet Union, engrained in Russians from the top to bottom. Even if Putin's immediate advisors assured him that the military was ready, he knew the consequences of the institutional structure he created. After all, he was once a part of the KGB and was briefly chief of the FSB—the same organization that was now assuring him that everything was fine.

While it would be easy to chalk up the mistake that Putin was about to make as a result of some sort of irrational behavior, the duller reality is that he likely just miscalculated. In the absence of clear information, he had to guess whether the intelligence was solid and the recommendation was wise. Few major decisions like this come without some level of risk. This was just one that happened to backfire spectacularly.

Further, from what we can observe, four factors pushed him in this direction, with perhaps a fifth subject to speculation.

First, with hindsight being 20/20, what he was about to try did not sound completely crazy at the time. Each of the three incorrect inferences he made—Western ambivalence, lack of Ukrainian resolve, and a strong Russian military—was plausible in February 2022. Indeed, these were common expectations within the media contemporaneously. Even Western opponents were not trying to convince Putin that the military portion of the invasion would fail, just that the international political consequences would not make it worthwhile.

Second, for the operation to truly backfire, Putin would have to encounter a confluence of bad luck. Specifically, the intelligence needed to steer him wrong on all three fronts simultaneously. Did Russia's military suffer from a variety of logistical problems? With the *vranyo* culture out there, maybe that was possible. Would the West actually pull together? Again, that was possible if the West was stalling assistance to Ukraine due to foot-dragging rather than indifference.

But if Ukraine quickly rolled over and folded like the Iraqi government did two decades earlier or the Afghan government did just six months previously, none of that would matter. The military would need to be engaged for more than a few weeks for any of the deep logistical problems to kill the invasion plans. Likewise, if the West had planned to provide aid, much of it would be irrelevant without a functional government in Kyiv. The West might just have to accept the new status quo, much as what happened following the capture of Crimea.

And if Russian intelligence were wrong about Zelensky, and Ukrainians stood by their leader and fought back? Obviously, that would be far from ideal for the Kremlin. But compared to Ukraine, Russia was still a much larger manufacturer of basically everything. The military assembly lines could make up the difference. Besides, with the slow rate of the Western response to the War in Donbas, Ukraine was lacking cutting-edge military equipment. The only way Russia could have a problem here would be if there were a third inaccurate conclusion. The West would need to shore up Ukraine's capacity. Simultaneously, those wealthy countries would need to lock down Russia's economy and limit the production of fresh weapons to use for the special military operation.

In other words, for Putin to encounter serious trouble with the invasion, the *pravda* needed to be that Russia's army was a paper tiger *and* that Ukraine would not simply concede due to indifference *and* that the West was willing to endure its own economic hardship that would come with supporting Ukraine's resistance. And even though all three of Russia's expectations were proven wrong, fast forwarding deep into the war's timeline, Russia would still control almost all of Luhansk, about half of Donetsk, the southern tier of Zaporizhzhia, and Kherson south of the Dnipro River.

It is possible that these errors were correlated. For example, conditional on miscalculating Ukrainian resolve, miscalculating the Western reaction was more likely. If a single intelligence report used the same assumptions to draw both conclusions simultaneously, then a disaster was more likely than it would first appear. But even still, from Putin's perspective, the odds of being wrong on all three at the same time were notably lower than being wrong on just one. In turn, Putin's miscalculation was not as egregious as it seems.

The third thing that could have sent Putin down the wrong path was the lack of blowback. Entering the war, it was unclear whether Putin would face serious repercussions if he were wrong about everything. Within the government, just about everyone was publicly onboard with the war. No obvious challengers to either the invasion decision or Putin's presidential office were in sight.

Indeed, the clearest manifestation of this came the day after Putin told his generals to make the final preparations for the war. Putin publicly convened a meeting of the Russian Security Council to discuss whether to recognize the independence of Luhansk and Donetsk. Advisor, after advisor, after advisor stood in front of the cameras to declare their support for the broader invasion effort. By doing so, each of them became at least partially culpable for whatever would happen next.

The climax of the meeting occurred when Director of the Foreign Intelligence Service Sergei Naryshkin approached the podium. As he gave his speech, Naryshkin appeared to slightly deviate from the party line. Putin hammered him. Following a couple of awkward exchanges, Naryshkin suggested that Russia outright annex Luhansk and Donetsk. Exasperated, Putin reminded Naryshkin that such a proposal was not *yet* on the agenda. One interpretation of this is that the Security Council previously discussed annexation as the endgame behind closed doors, and Narhyshkin momentarily forgot where they were in the script. Eventually, Naryshkin got back onto message. He, like everyone else, was now publicly on board.

Putin had achieved his goal. Public opinion polling of Putin was fairly high going into the war, even according to independent polling firms. He was popular, even if some of that popularity was attributable to the strict control he had over Russian media. Regardless, following the Security Council meeting, he now had an endless supply of scapegoats if he ever wanted to pull out. Scapegoats would not guarantee his political survival under those circumstances, but it was better for him to have that option than not.

The fourth issue was the COVID-19 pandemic. Given the stakes, Putin naturally would have wanted to verify for himself as much information as he could. Under normal circumstances, the state's institutions should do that on his behalf. But that ship had sailed. Putin's own effort here would have been a vital stop-gap measure.

However, the pandemic killed any such plans. Apparently worried about catching COVID, Putin limited his travel schedule. Prior to the pandemic, he frequently oversaw training exercises and visited military facilities. Had that continued during the pandemic, he might have spotted more cracks in the system or heard from dissenting voices that normally could not reach the Kremlin. Instead, Putin stayed to himself. Retreating to Sochi exacerbated the problem, placing further distance between him and the malfunctioning bureaucracy.

The speculative final issue is Putin's health. Rumors that Putin struggles with some type of long-term or perhaps terminal illness have circulated since the start of his presidency. Ukrainian intelligence sometimes stokes the flames by explicitly promoting the claim. The publicly available evidence for this is scant but enough to keep the rumor mill running. And if true, it would further explain why Putin was too busy to verify the intelligence reports he received.

The health saga began from the start of Putin's presidency, as commentators noticed that he had an interesting way of walking. Putin clearly favors his right side, with a shallow stride and keeping the corresponding arm frozen. Many observers call this a "gunslinger's gait," suggesting that Putin learned it during his time in the KGB. According to this theory, the apparent limp was actually designed to give him quick access to a sidearm. Ostensibly, Putin became so accustomed to the motion that it has outlasted his time actually carrying a gun.

All of this speculation traces back to a single KGB handbook. It indeed does recommend a gait similar to how Putin walks. However, the instructions are only for when the agent is in an active combat situation, specifically under the heading "Special Features of Night Movement." It was *not* intended as a general mandate. This makes sense—if every KGB agent walked like that under all circumstances, the FBI and CIA would have marked all of them with little effort. It is also unclear how much time Putin spent in the field as a KGB agent versus working more bureaucratic tasks. Thus, the limp may not be intentional but rather is a product of some underlying health condition.

Another piece of the puzzle is Putin's "moon-shaped face." This is something that evolved over his time in office. The condition gets its name from how the afflicted individual's face becomes noticeably round and bloated. Its common causes are prolonged use of steroids or cortisol, meaning that this could be a side effect of a treatment he is receiving for a more serious condition. Comparing photos of Putin today to when he first came into office, there is a distinct change. At the same time, everyone's face evolves over the decades, so the true cause is unclear.

The third clue is social distance. During the pandemic, Putin would sit far away from almost all of his public guests.

This included the fateful Security Council meeting, where each of his advisors sat across from him inside a large atrium. But the world is most familiar with this from the final East-West pre-war negotiations. Both French President Emmanuel Macron and German Chancellor Olaf Scholz made separate trips to Moscow and sat across from Putin at a comically large table. Photos from those meetings would come to symbolize the yawning gap in their world outlooks. In terms of the health question, the speculation here is that Putin was afraid of catching COVID due to comorbidities. This would further rationalize the other steps he took during the pandemic.

The armchair diagnosing accelerated shortly after the war began. People noticed that Putin adopted a habit of grabbing tables with his right hand. He turns his palm to face upward, grabs the underside of the table with his four fingers, and secures the grip with his thumb on the top. It does not look comfortable. The speculation is that grabbing the table allows Putin to control a tremble or relieve pain by engaging his muscles. He also taps his feet while sitting, causing speculation that he does this for the same reason he grabs the table.

Some of the armchair diagnosing was completely misguided. One theory suggested that a doctor follows Putin around at all times in case of a medical emergency. This is true but mundane. A doctor also follows the U.S. president around because it is a sensible policy decision for any country with vast resources. Others pointed to Putin holding onto a blanket during the May 9 Victory Day parade, despite ostensibly warm weather. However, he was not alone in doing this. Moreover, the blankets are a bit of military legend—they were a key part of the Soviet Union's survival strategy against Nazi Germany's siege.

In sum, there is a limp, a moon-shaped face, extra cautious social distancing, a hand grab, and a foot tap. It is not quite a conspiracy theory, but the evidence is far from conclusive.

Regardless, Putin believed that the attack would likely be successful. And even if the operation failed to live up to its fullest potential, the fallback possibilities still looked good. With that, he pulled the trigger. The invasion would begin at dawn on February 24.

The Battle of Kyiv

Over the first two months of 2022, President Zelensky must have had frequent sleepless nights as his mind focused on a potential war. On February 24, he awoke well before sunrise to the news he feared: Russia's invasion had begun. By 5:30 am, he had met with his National Security and Defense Council and declared martial law. The war was not just an escalation of the Donbas conflict from the last eight years. Nor was it just on the border regions between Russia and Ukraine. It was *everywhere*.

The lead vehicles of the dreaded Russian Kyiv Convoy reached the capital shortly thereafter. The 64 kilometers of materiel that were primed to follow represented the seemingly inevitable end of the Ukrainian state. Pockets of fighting were already active around Kyiv. From the presidential palace, Zelensky could do little more than organize what seemed like a final stand against the Russian invasion.

With the battle on his doorstep, Western partners offered to evacuate Zelensky from the country. Once he reached a safer location—say, Poland, under the protection of NATO's security guarantees—Zelensky could establish a government in exile. The international community would continue to recognize him as the sovereign leader of Ukraine even after Kyiv fell. And if insurgents succeeded in driving out the Russian invaders, he could return to the country and reinitiate a normal governance.

But that is not the route Zelensky took. As the Ukrainian embassy in the United Kingdom tells the story, Zelensky responded by declaring "The fight is here. I need ammunition not a ride." Although perhaps apocryphal, the story stuck. It became a rallying call to fight for the survival of the Ukrainian state.

However, to outside observers, including the U.S. intelligence community, it appeared that ammunition was the least of Ukraine's concerns. What Zelensky really needed was a miracle.

At the time, Russia was the consensus pick for the second or third greatest military power in the world, behind only the United States and perhaps China. Ukrainian strength was a drop in the bucket by comparison. Kyiv was massively outgunned, and the bulk of the convoy was only 150 kilometers away from the presidential palace. Under normal circumstances, that is a distance a civilian could drive in less than two hours. And while the circumstances that day were anything but normal, Russia's strategic planners had set midnight as the latest time that Russian troops should reach the capital. Three days later, the battle was supposed to be over. U.S. estimates suggested that it might take a few more days than that, but such a distinction hardly put any Ukrainian minds at ease.

Despite that, Ukraine would survive the first day. Then the second. Then a week. By March 11, the dreaded convoy had dispersed, apparently more interested in taking cover than taking Kyiv. By March 16, Ukraine would begin a true counterattack. By March 29, Russia would announce its plan to depart from the area, ending the western offensive entirely.

But this was no miracle. It was a combination of Ukrainian ingenuity and Russian missteps that prevented Moscow from achieving its goal.

Russian Mobilization

Speaking about the 2003 Iraq War, U.S. Secretary of Defense Donald Rumsfeld famously quipped that "You go to war with the army you have, not the army you might want." Rumsfeld was correct in the broadest sense. For instance, a country cannot magically will nuclear weapons into existence as much as it might wish. However, that sentiment understates the amount of control that a country's leadership has. Leaders decide how much effort they and their populations exert in a conflict, and those choices influence the quality of military outcomes.

As a starting point, a leader could go with low effort. The tomahawk cruise missile campaign and no fly zone that NATO established over Libya during the 2011 civil war is a good example of this. Politically inactive citizens at home might not even be aware there is any military action taking place. The participating governments must pay the price for deployment, ammunition, and normal wear and tear, but the risk to equipment and soldiers' lives is minimal.

Then there is medium effort, like the Iraq War that Rumsfeld oversaw. The United States actually put boots on the ground. Many died. Conflicts like these become major news stories at home, and they put a notable dent in a state's budget. But they still only require a volunteer force, and they do not cause massive economic distortions.

Next up is high effort. The Vietnam War is emblematic of this. Now conscription becomes necessary to sustain the fight because the corresponding military strategies entail higher combat fatalities. At least some level of domestic unrest is inevitable. The war will not only be the centerpiece of the country's foreign policy, but it might dominate the domestic political debates as well.

At the top end is the all-in war effort. World War II is the perfect case study. The entirety of the country's focus shifts to the war. Basically everyone's labor, even those not directly involved in the fighting, is somehow eventually connected to the broader war plan. Yearly war spending totals a double-digit percentage of the country's gross domestic product. Major social changes that were previously inconceivable—like women entering the workforce—become a necessity.

Toward the end of 2021, deep inside the halls of the Kremlin, Vladimir Putin was thinking about where to place Russia on this spectrum. As the examples indicated, military mobilizations are political decisions that come with costs and benefits. The obvious benefit is that the more a country mobilizes, the more likely that country is to win a war. As it relates to the conflict at hand, that meant a higher chance that more of Ukraine would fall into Russian hands.

The downside is that the more the country mobilizes, the greater the costs it incurs to do so. The government must recruit and pay any additional soldiers it deploys. Further, those soldiers leave the workforce, lowering tax revenues and generally decreasing the country's economic efficiency. On the political side, the country's leader is more likely to face challenges to the regime. This can come both from disgruntled citizens who do not want to deploy abroad as well as oligarchs that do not want to see their profits diminish. These concerns go double in the case of a regime like Russia's, as failed autocrats are much more likely to face exile, jail, or death in their post-tenure fates than democratic leaders are.

Regardless, the overall goal for a country's leader is to find the mobilization level where the additional economic costs and political risks exactly offset the additional chance of victory. At that point, the leader is doing the best they can given the circumstances they face.

Putin, it turns out, calculated that a medium mobilization was his best choice, most comparable to the Iraq War example from earlier. Factors on both sides of the equation led to that conclusion. On the military side, the intelligence problems described in the previous chapter now came into play. Given estimates of the Russian army's abilities and expectations that Ukraine was unwilling to fight, the Kremlin believed that every soldier mobilized would hit hard.

A basic military rule of thumb is that troops on the offensive need a roughly three-to-one numerical advantage to overcome defensive entrenchments. The specific ratio varies from case to case, depending on training, equipment, the extent of defensive preparation, and whether the conflict will take place in open fields or if urban combat is the order of the day. Regardless, Russia's plan did not come close to the guidelines. Ukraine was expected to field 200,000 troops to defend against the initial invasion. Between its own forces and those coming from the Donbas, Russia ultimately mobilized about the same quantity.

The Kremlin's military planners were not naïve here. Rather, under this theory, raising a gigantic army was overkill. A small operation like the Libya intervention would not cut it—Russia needed to put troops on the ground. And there needed to be some heft behind it, as levels like what Moscow used in the shadow conflict in the Donbas would not be sufficient. But Vietnam levels of mobilization—never mind World War II levels—were absurd to suggest if most Ukrainians were just going to quit once Russia arrived.

On the political side, such massive mobilizations would come with domestic costs. It is easy to use the word "autocrat" to shorthand Putin's position prior to the war. But his situation was different than other famous autocrats like Josef Stalin, Saddam Hussein, or Kim Jong-un. Those leaders succeeded in completely centralizing power. Putin had undermined democratic processes, but some Russian institutions still existed. Any mobilization he proposed would have to navigate through them. And the larger the mobilization Putin asked for, the more challenging it would be.

Russian citizens were not oblivious to how Putin had steadily eroded democratic norms since he came to power on December 31, 1999. Nor were they pleased about it. Although Putin himself was popular, surveys still showed that Russians preferred competitive elections and rule of law. They were just willing to look the other way—either because they did not mind Putin serving additional terms or because resisting would be too costly.

Moreover, the implicit bargain that Putin had offered the Russian people was acceptable. As long as oil prices remained high, the economy was booming. The average Russian was doing much better during the Putin era than during Yeltsin's post-Soviet transition period. If that continued indefinitely, and Putin's foreign affairs were not affecting the daily lives of those in the Russian Federation, they left him free to pursue his own agenda. A similar principle applied to the oligarch class—they could get rich and maintain their business empires so long as they stayed out of politics.

In fact, part of Putin's popularity stemmed from his reforms in separating foreign affairs from the everyday lives of Russians. Russia transitioned from a system with two years of mandatory conscription to half of that. Furthermore, only a third of those eligible ultimately served, thanks in large part to bribes or political connections. By 2019, the Kremlin had declared its intention to end conscription altogether and move to a professional military. Russians—particularly the politically important ones in Saint Petersburg and Moscow—would not have to think twice about the international politics around them. They may have faced some indirect costs of conflict through higher taxation or sanctions. But the only people who would risk their lives would be those agreeing to receive a wage in return.

This, in part, is why the War in Donbas up until 2022 looked the way it did. Rather than engage in a traditional invasion, Russia sent unmarked soldiers into Eastern Ukraine to foment a separatist movement. The smaller footprint meant that men on the streets of Moscow did not wonder whether they would find themselves in their Near Abroad on short notice. More generally, the law restricted the service of conscripted soldiers to within Russia's borders during peacetime. That meant Putin had limited options: invade with only contracted soldiers, make a very public declaration of war, or try to sneak around the system.

In sum, Putin's sensitivity on the political risk meter was higher than how it appeared from the outside. Thus, Putin announced a "special military operation" on the morning of February 24. A "war" mobilization would have a specific legal meaning and raise more alarm bells across the country than he wanted to. And given Ukraine's apparently weak position, all of that was supposed to be unnecessary. Putin could have gone for more—and indeed would later. But to have done so at the time seemed like a waste.

Operational Secrecy: Good for Russia

The smaller footprint Putin sought had a second apparent advantage: operational secrecy. The Russian president was committed to starting the war. But he was not about to publicize those desires—especially to Western audiences.

Recall from two chapters ago that the West offered a discombobulated response to the growing invasion threat. The United States, United Kingdom, and Baltic States were convinced that Russia was going to make a move. However, Ukraine believed that Russia's implicit threats were not inherently credible. Many within Continental Europe shared this assessment.

Most importantly, Germany and France were concerned over Washington's escalation in rhetoric. They still felt burned after the 2003 Iraq War. Two decades earlier, U.S. intelligence officials far overplayed their hands, claiming confidence about Saddam Hussein's alleged weapons of mass destruction program. Germany and France both vocalized their opposition to the conflict, and the subsequent invasion vindicated their decision.

The schism was primarily the George W. Bush administration's fault, of course. Obama, Trump, and Biden had resided in the West Wing in the meantime, but 2021 raised a new source of doubt for the European powers. The United States had insisted that Afghanistan's government would hold for a reasonable period after the American withdrawal. Instead, it seemingly evaporated overnight. France and Germany were left to wonder what made the accuracy of this U.S. intelligence report any different. Until they had confirmation, Paris and Berlin were content to maintain a guarded relationship, calculating that Putin's blustering would not go beyond the implicit threats.

As a result, Putin's goal was to continue the diplomatic charade for as long as he could. Although he was optimistic that Europe's ultimate response would not go beyond a few slaps on the wrist, he wanted to delay any trouble as far into the future as possible. Moreover, had Russia's military achieved a lightning victory as anticipated, there would have been little for the West to do regardless. The hope was to create a repeat of Crimea in 2014.

The secrecy plot worked, even late in the game. Despite U.S. intelligence leaking Russia's next moves on a regular basis, still no consensus formed in the West about what would happen in the days to come. France in particular worked hard to bridge the negotiations. President Emmanuel Macron flew to Moscow on February 7. He failed to come to an understanding with Putin, but this did yield the photos of them sitting at the absurdly long table. Chancellor Olaf Scholz repeated that process a week later.

Undeterred, Macron's efforts continued for one more week. This time, it was a phone call on February 20, for a final shot at diplomacy. By the end of the conversation, Macron was convinced that Putin still sought a peaceful solution. In retrospect, Putin's priorities were telling. He ended the call early so he could head to an ice rink and play hockey.

Everything fell apart from there. The next day, Putin traded his ice skates for a pen, signing documents to officially recognize the independence of Donetsk and Luhansk. Three days after that, the special military operation began.

Operational Secrecy: Bad for Russia

Unfortunately for Russian military planners, keeping the secret for that length of time came with some serious tradeoffs for the organization of the invasion. Problems arose from the top to the bottom of the chain of command.

It is possible that even the most senior Russian officials were kept in the dark regarding the invasion until the final moments. Hoping to deter the Kremlin, on November 2, 2021, Biden dispatched CIA Director William Burns to Moscow. This was the same trip mentioned earlier where the Russian military leadership claimed that all of corruption and waste were the problems of yesteryear. But when he met with Nikolai Patrushev, Secretary of the Russian Security Council, he had a completely different experience. By some estimates, Patrushev was a frontrunner to take control of the Kremlin if Putin were to ever step down. Burns' goal was to warn him that the United States was prepared to respond in force if Russia invaded.

However, after Burns rattled off his list of potential consequences, Patrushev just responded with shock. Burns was unsure how to interpret this. A natural first reaction would be to conclude that Patrushev was working on his acting skills. That is, he was in on the plan, but did not want to give the CIA chief any confirmation of Putin's endgame. But that was not how Burns interpreted the events. Instead, he estimated that Patrushev was learning and processing all of this information in real time.

U.S. Secretary of State Antony Blinken had a similar experience. In January 2022, Blinken toured Europe with the lingering threat of war on his mind. His first stop on the 19th was to Kyiv to meet with his Ukrainian counterpart, Dmytro Kuleba. After a brief stop in Germany, he boarded his plane to fly to Geneva. There, he would meet with Russian Minister of Foreign Affairs Sergey Lavrov on the 21st.

For an hour and a half, Blinken pressed Lavrov for answers regarding Russia's intentions. Lavrov responded by talking in circles, apparently confused by the accusations. Like Burns before him, Blinken was unsure of what to make of the situation. Again, perhaps Lavrov was acting. But Blinken left the meeting uncertain which of the two diplomats was better informed about Putin's actual plans.

Behind the scenes, Putin's goals were ambitious. Whether his intention was a full annexation of the country is unclear. At a minimum, there were plans to create a new government in Kyiv, either as a vassal state or to create a legal framework for Ukraine to "voluntarily" reunite with Moscow. In particular, the FSB eyed three potential succession plans should Zelensky's government fall. The straightforward solution was Viktor Yanukovych, the former Ukrainian president who had fled to Russia in 2014 during the Maidan Revolution. On March 7, 2022, his plane flew to Belarus, apparently positioning itself to quickly arrive in Kyiv. It is unknown whether Yanukovych was on board. But assuming he was, he could have flown into the capital had Russian troops secured control. Yanukovych could have then staked a claim as the legitimate leader of Ukraine, arguing that his 2014 removal came via extralegal means.

A second plan was to use a televised message from Yanukovych to anoint Viktor Medvedchuk as his successor. Medvedchuk had earlier served multiple spells within the Ukrainian Rada as a pro-Russian voice. He further had a close relationship with Putin, to the extent that Putin is his daughter's godfather. However, since 2021, Medvedchuk had been under house arrest stemming from charges of treason and corruption. Within two days of the start of the invasion, though, he mysteriously disappeared. It took Ukrainian officials two months to track him down.

The third plot arose from Ukraine's southeast. This involved Oleg Tsaryov, another former member of the

Ukrainian Rada. Following the Maidan Revolution, he led the brief "New Russia" movement, which sought to create a confederacy of Luhansk, Donetsk, and other oblasts. The "others" failed to materialize, and the movement faded into obscurity within a year. But Russia's invasion aimed to breathe new life into Tsaryov's plans.

However, none of this appears to have filtered down to the Russian troops who would be responsible for implementing any of it. Under the impression that they were in Belarus for training exercises, Russian troops had little reason to depart from the traditional corruption that plagued their ranks. Members of tank groups would find having a well-functioning tank critical if they believed they were about to enter hostile territory. But the Kremlin had deliberately kept them in the dark on that. And when one of these soldiers does not believe the maintenance of their tank is the difference between life and death, it becomes a miniature gold mine. Copper wiring, diesel fuel, and armored plating all fetch good money on the black market. Within an instant, millions of dollars in equipment would become worthless because a Russian soldier just wanted a few rubles to buy some vodka. In short, the *vranyo* culture was alive and well among the deployed.

Eventually, high-level Russian leadership had to inform the soldiers of what was happening. But for many, the forewarning was between one day and just one *hour*—not enough time to undo weeks, months, or years of damage due to corruption.

The lack of preparation showed. Some soldiers were given simple instructions: follow the vehicle in front of you, and you will reach the capital as early as mid-afternoon. Contingency plans—for example, what would happen if one of those vehicles were to break down or blow up—were not outlined. Many did not know where to go. In the worst instance of this, near Chernobyl, Russian troops marched through the red forest, so named because of the color the trees turned to after absorbing radiation. Worse yet, there are indications that they dug trenches in the area, exposing themselves to the radiation still contained in the ground.

Rather than receiving the world's most advanced military technology, soldiers lacked even the most basic tools of the trade. One Russian soldier was discovered with a Wikipedia printout with instructions on how to use his weapon. Outdated maps of Ukraine harkening back to the 1960s were discovered on others. Without dedicated lines of radio communications, soldiers used their own cell phones, giving away their locations to the enemy. Medics received an undersupply of provisions, perhaps linked to expectations that the war would be easy. Many received instructions to pack their dress uniforms instead of the food and water they would soon need.

At a higher level, Russia could not conduct a shock and awe campaign in the style of the United States prior to the Iraq War. The point of such campaigns is to simplify the army's responsibilities. Had key parts of Ukraine already been on fire, invading soldiers could have spent more time mopping things up than doing the heavy lifting. Targeting anti-aircraft systems ahead of time would have given Russian aircraft greater freedom, which could have further protected the ground-based soldiers.

As alluded to earlier, the problem with such a deliberate approach is that it would have delayed the expected time between the start of kinetic efforts and the capture of Kyiv. In the meantime, it would have clarified the rest of the world's perceptions of the Kremlin's intentions. France and Germany would have had no choice but to conclude that the U.S. intelligence estimates were correct. Their true pressure campaign would have then begun shortly thereafter.

Meanwhile, Russian troops could not simply stay in Belarus forever. The claim that the soldiers were there to conduct exercises would have begun to ring hollow as days turned to weeks turned to months. This was also the second time that Russia had mobilized to Belarus, after having sent tens of thousands of troops there in the winter and spring of 2021. To depart and then return for a third time would have raised suspicions.

Ready or not, this was the Russian invasion force that would head toward Kyiv.

The Ticking Time Bomb

By outward appearances, Ukraine was outgunned. But inside Kyiv, there was more than a sliver of hope. The key was in Ukrainian intelligence estimates of what Russia could do past the initial few days of an invasion. The aforementioned cross-border intelligence raid was key to this. Finding drunk units and rusting tanks meant that Ukraine had a chance. Knowing that plans for any possible invasion were not reaching the soldiers responsible for implementing it further meant that there was an opportunity. Russia's invasion force was a ticking time bomb. But rather than being one about to explode on the capital, it was ticking down to its own self-destruction.

All Ukraine needed to do to be competitive in the war was to survive the first 72 hours. At that point, Russian soldiers would begin running out of food and fuel. Equipment would start to break down. And without any contingency plans put into place, most of the special military operation would begin to flail around.

Ukraine would not be guaranteed to win the war, of course. Nor could Kyiv be assured about anything happening on its eastern borders or near the Crimean Peninsula. Eventually, Russia would have an opportunity to regroup, organize properly, and perhaps mount a real invasion. But a good game plan at a minimum could keep Kyiv in the hands of Ukraine. With enough damage inflicted on Russia, it might remove the capital from contention entirely.

All told, Kyiv's gameplan had five components: (1) prevent Russia from establishing a sky bridge into Kyiv, (2) keep Zelensky alive and in the country, (3) render the Russian Air Force ineffective, (4) repel the initial attack on the capital, and (5) make the convoy regret ever having crossed the Belarusian border.

This book's opening chapter covered the first point, with Ukraine's defense of the Hostomel Airport. But the rest remained open questions even after the early successes there.

Zelensky: The Modern-Day Winston Churchill

Of the four remaining points, keeping Zelensky alive and in the country was the easiest to fulfill. Moreover, the "in the country" part was a gimme. All Zelensky had to do was refuse any plane, train, or automobile that the West was offering to escape the country. Nevertheless, it took a calculated gamble on his part to follow through. The rest of Ukraine's plan was far from a guaranteed success. And as the Russian army approached Kyiv, it would become increasingly difficult for Zelensky to flee. The spillover effects would be devastating: the continuity of Ukraine's government would be put in jeopardy, and his capture or death would facilitate the appointment of a Russian proxy to the presidency.

As Zelensky awoke in the middle of the night to the invasion underway, his initial task was to meet with defense ministers to address where he should go. They reached a quick consensus: Zelensky should stay in Kyiv. Part of the rapid collapse of Afghanistan's government was the result of President Ashraf Ghani's departure on August 15, 2021. At that point, even enlisted Afghan soldiers and high-ranking officers sympathetic to democracy calculated that they had nothing left to play for, resulting in mass dereliction. If Zelensky left, Ukraine might repeat that experience.

In contrast, if Zelensky stayed, he could inspire a rally 'round the flag effect. Average Ukrainians might become motivated to stay and fight as well. To underscore that point, Zelensky emerged from hiding onto the streets of Kyiv, declaring his intention to stay and fight and pleading for others to do the same. Even as the bombs rained down, he could inspire and mobilize the masses, just as Winston Churchill did for the United Kingdom throughout Nazi Germany's Blitz during World War II. The higher chances of a complete success in repelling Russia's invasion justified the higher personal risks to Zelensky.

However, keeping Zelensky alive required a strategy that went beyond simply staying still. Even if he could militarily win the Battle of Kyiv, Zelensky still had to worry about assassination attempts on the ground and from the sky. The ground part was the bigger concern. It was a major component of CIA Director Burns' message to Zelensky, warning the president of specific plots that Russia might use. Just a few days prior to the invasion, U.S. Vice President Kamala Harris reiterated those warnings to Zelensky at the Munich Security Conference. Other leaders there suggested that he simply not return to Kyiv.

It was not just the possibility that Russia might drop special forces into the capital to specifically target Zelensky. At least Ukraine could defend against that by keeping Zelensky's location a secret and by assigning the properly sized security detail. Rather, defections were a recurring problem across the country. Had a single person within Zelensky's own security service turned, Russia could have taken down the president from the inside. Ukraine therefore retooled its protection assignments: only those whose loyalty was unquestionable could get near Zelensky while armed.

Of course, that would not stop Moscow from raining bombs from above to accomplish the same goal. Ironically, however, Moscow had sabotaged that plan decades earlier.

Much of Kyiv's infrastructure was a byproduct of Cold War planning. Across the country, subway tunnels that were normally meant for trains were built deeper underground to double as nuclear fallout shelters. During the initial stages of the invasion, civilians jammed inside them for safety.

But the Office of the President had an even better option: a large bunker system under Kyiv specifically designed to keep the government functioning from below. Zelensky was now using what was originally intended to prevent U.S. nuclear weapons from eradicating the Soviet government as an alternative to Washington's invitation to leave the country. Those who have been inside the bunker tunnels describe them as so vast and disorienting that even if you knew where Zelensky was within them, you would have a hard time navigating your way there.

When it was safe, Zelensky popped out every now and then to record another video. Sustaining the rally 'round the flag effect was important, and he could put his skills as a former actor to great use. It also provided verification to the Ukrainian people that he was still alive. But the bunker network effectively guaranteed his safety. And just like that, Ukraine had foiled one of the critical components of Russia's invasion plans.

Halt the Russian Air Force

After having stopped Russia from establishing an airbase at Hostomel, Ukraine faced a more general task of keeping the skies competitive. Military planners in Kyiv succeeded here due to a combination of Russian rigidity, Ukrainian foresight, and a little help from some friends.

In the months prior to the war, Ukraine dispersed its anti-aircraft systems as a preliminary step toward creating a more robust defense network. Planners were fully aware that Russia would want to target them to clear a path for the Russian air force and needed to find a way to keep them safe. Movement was the solution. In the days before the actual invasion, Ukraine further reshuffled many of its systems. And they kept reshuffling as the days continued.

Although time consuming, this was the correct counterplay. Ukrainian traitors had given away the original positions. However, Russia did not receive any updates as the first wave of strikes began. As a result, the majority of the first wave missed their intended targets, instead hitting empty spaces. To make matters worse for Russia, Russian pilots were briefly under the false impression that the opening strikes were an unmitigated success. As such, they flew without caution. Ukraine was all too happy to treat that period as open season.

Eventually, Russian intelligence noticed that the initial strikes had missed and looked for a way to hunt down the rotating locations. Sometimes the searchers were successful. Nevertheless, Russia still faced a problem in acting on the intelligence. The excessively bureaucratic nature of the Russian military meant that two or three days might pass between the acquisition of the intelligence and the actual attack. In turn, as long as Ukraine kept cycling locations, the anti-aircraft systems could stay mostly intact.

Despite having an inferior air force with a substantially worse range, Ukrainian planes also got into the act. Ukraine noticed that many Russian bombers would fly alone, without anti-aircraft fighter jets acting as escorts. The Ukrainian pilots discovered that they could fly their ostensibly inferior planes low to the ground, hidden from Russian radar, and ambush Russian bombers.

Russia eventually got wise to Ukraine's strategy. The counter-counterplay was to fly Russian bombers low as well, also preventing Ukrainian radar from detecting them. However, Ukraine was ready with a counter-counter-counterplay. Low flying aircraft are vulnerable to man-portable air-defense systems, or MANPADS. In January 2022, Zelensky found a windfall of MANPADS from the United States and Europe, and now Ukraine had trapped the Russian planes in a place where Ukraine could put the systems to their full use. As a result, what appeared to be a clear aircraft advantage to Russia on paper ended up being manageable for Ukraine.

But Ukraine's most difficult tasks were yet to come.

Repelling Russia's Initial Attack

Ukraine still had to worry about the traditional ground assault. The preliminary phase was stopping the oncoming rush of Russian soldiers. Then Kyiv could worry about the larger stream of materiel that Russia planned to force into the capital.

In broad strokes, Ukraine divided the workflow in two, setting up an outer ring and an inner ring of defense around the city. The purpose of the inner ring was to serve as a possible last stand. It encompassed all the major portions of the capital, stretching northwest near Hostomel. If all else failed, Ukraine could take the battle to the streets and force Russia into urban combat. Russia might still have the ability to overpower Ukrainian resistance, but it would require going from building to building to clear out enemy forces.

However, Ukraine knew what this could do to a city. Russia fought two wars against Chechnya, a separatist region in the Northern Caucasus portion of the Russian Federation. Grozny, its capital, spent years under siege, the target of endless artillery strikes and armored columns. By the end, its infrastructure was gutted. Grozny's population declined from 400,000 in 1989 to 211,000 in 2002.

Thus, Ukraine established an outer ring, radiating toward both suburban and rural areas, and reaching close to the Belarusian border to the north. Keeping Russia outside its perimeter was unlikely. Nevertheless, the point was to begin engagements far away from the Kyiv city center. Both the government and its economic hub were at stake. Ukraine not only wanted to win the battle—it wanted to save its capital city.

Ukrainian defenders on the outer ring had a strategic advantage: Russia was splitting its attack. There was the Kyiv front, which has occupied the focus of all these pages so far. But some of the 200,000 Russian invaders were on the Eastern front, and yet more of them were south on the Crimean front. (These will be the subject of the next chapter.) Ukraine had to post defenders at these other locations too. In fact, Kyiv anticipated that Russia's main attack would occur out of the Donbas, essentially escalating the long-running conflict in terms of force but not purpose. As Russian troops poured into the capital, Ukraine recalled some of those soldiers. It was a difficult tradeoff but a necessary one. Kyiv essentially exchanged land elsewhere for the capital's survival. After all, had the government fallen, the rest of Ukraine might have toppled over like a line of dominoes.

The other way Ukraine could shift the force ratios was to simply enlarge the resistance force. Kyiv opened up its armories, inviting average Ukrainian citizens to take military-grade weapons. Ordinary people had been doing this unofficially since Russia's shadow war in the Donbas began in 2014. In a fortunate coincidence in timing, Zelensky signed into law the creation of the Territorial Defense Force in July 2021. This would organize an official reserve system, which just so happened to begin service on January 1, 2022.

Meanwhile, regular civilians disconnected from the reserves also helped out. They began converting every empty glass bottle in the city into Molotov cocktails. These are normal breakable containers, like a discarded beer bottle, filled with a flammable liquid. In emergency situations like what Ukraine faced, gasoline is a common substance due to its wide availability. A cloth doused in the liquid goes on top. When ready, the user lights the cloth and throws the Molotov cocktail at the target. The glass bottle shatters, rapidly igniting the area. The fact that the name is derived from Finland's resistance against Moscow's invasion during the Winter War of 1939—and referencing the Soviet Foreign Minister Vyacheslav Molotov—was not lost on the Ukrainians.

These actions had two side benefits. First, had conventional Ukrainian defenses failed, Russia would have been stuck facing a well-armed insurgency. The United States knows all too well how that plays out. Two decades earlier, after having emerged victorious in the traditional militarized conflict portion of the Iraq War, the United States sent home all of Saddam Hussein's former soldiers. They understood that the government that was soon to form would treat them as an "out" group. But they took their guns home with them, which meant that their insurgency began with a significant head start. Whatever form of government Russia might institute in Kyiv, Western-oriented Ukrainians had a similar expectation. Ample guns meant that the fight could continue in some form even if the government ceased to exist.

Second, it would force low-level politicians to think twice about collaborating with Russia. Any mayor considering whether to welcome Russian troops had to worry that dozens of their neighbors might arrive at city hall, angry and armed to the teeth. Defections were a bigger problem in the east, and such weapons might not stop any true-believer turncoats. But it would force anyone thinking of becoming a political entrepreneur to carefully consider the decision. Given that the fall of one town can precipitate the fall of the next, even small nudges like this were helpful.

Meanwhile, as the defenders in an urban combat environment, Ukraine enjoyed some significant tactical advantages. Invading soldiers were stuck having to advance on the streets. But for Ukraine, every building was a potential ambush point or sniper's nest. In their three-day rush to take the capital, Russian soldiers faced a tradeoff. Option one was to go full speed ahead and risk life and limb. Option two was to take a deliberate approach, clear the streets building by building, and eventually control the entire city.

In principle, the first option sounded reasonable. Russia's theory of victory was that Ukrainian resistance would fall apart once invading soldiers had disbanded Kyiv's government. Blazing through the streets might give the defending soldiers an opportunity to try hitting tanks, armored personnel carriers, and dismounted soldiers. But the moment would be fleeting. If the first shots missed, Russian troops would already be at the next block over. In contrast, going building by building would guarantee sustained engagements and the casualties to match.

However, Ukraine took part of that decision out of Russia's hands. The key here was an anti-tank obstacle known as a Czech hedgehog. Its design is simple. Take three metal I-beams roughly two meters in length. Then weld them together at their center points, so that each beam is pointed in a different direction. The result is a structure with six endpoints in total, shaped like children's toy jacks. No matter how you set it down or how it rolls afterward, it rests on a tripod. Their origins date back to World War II, and the beaches of Normandy are littered with them in classic photographs from D-Day. The first half of the name comes from their invention to fortify Czechoslovakia's border with Nazi Germany.

There is perhaps no better way to stall a tank than with a Czech hedgehog. If any vehicle attempts to roll up to a hedgehog, the device is liable to lodge itself under the vehicle's chassis and lift it off the ground. Hedgehogs will not destroy tanks by themselves. But their advantage over alternative obstacles like landmines is durability. Once a tank unit sees a minefield, the unit can deploy countermeasures to rapidly detonate all of the mines and continue forward. In contrast, soldiers cannot blast their way through Czech hedgehogs. Explosives will only turn the hedgehog to another side. But they are designed so that no matter how they are resting, there is still a tripod on the ground and still a tripod facing upward. This explains the second half of their name—Czech hedgehogs are pointy and can spin around, just like the animal. Destroying them is not an option. Instead, the best a blast can do is move them far enough to open up a space for the tanks to pass through. Even then, hedgehogs weigh roughly 200 kilograms. Moving one requires a lot of ordinance, and defenders may place multiple layers at key strategic intersections.

This leaves two options. First is to manually move them. Their enormous weight means that muscle strength alone is not adequate. To shift them in any time-efficient manner, an invading army needs to attach a cable to each hedgehog and tow them a few meters to clear a lane. Under normal circumstances, this would be an inconvenience. However, in the middle of a war in an urban setting, it is a nightmare. While soldiers fiddle around with tow cables, any building in sight might be a sniper's nest. The tanks are also stalled during that time, making them easy targets for anti-tank munitions.

The second option is to go around. That is a better alternative when the theater of combat is an open field, which defined much of the fighting in the Donbas and Crimean fronts. The Kyiv front was a different story. Dense cities do not provide an immediate alternative—there is a road, and on either side of it are buildings. The tanks cannot blast their way through concrete structures—not without expending ridiculous quantities of explosives. Thus, either the invaders need to clear the hedgehogs or find another street and hope that it does not have the same obstacles.

The broader geography of central Ukraine caused further problems. Due to the endless rivers and hills, bridges are a critical part of Ukrainian infrastructure. But they create natural choke points—going around them is not a feasible option because it might mean dozens of extra kilometers of travel. Correspondingly, Ukraine flooded these locations with hedgehogs, daring Russian soldiers to expose themselves while attempting to clear a path. The threat of ambush alone was a deterrent. Consequently, Ukraine did not need to create ambush points along every Czech hedgehog trapping to still enjoy some of the benefits.

Fortunately for Ukraine, production of Czech hedgehogs was not an issue. All someone needs are three I-beams and welding experience. As soon as the war began, welders across Ukraine quit what they were doing, found whatever scrap metal was lying around, and mass produced them. Ironically, the act of war itself made the acquisition step easier—as more buildings were destroyed, more raw materials for I-beams suddenly became available. They are also incredibly durable, to the point where there are stories that Ukraine pulled some out of World War II museums, still as functional as ever.

Nevertheless, pockets of Russian soldiers did penetrate into the city, leading to full-on urban combat. The closest call occurred early on February 26, when Russian invaders approached the Kyiv Zoo, right along the city's main artery. Had they continued down that road, they were less than seven kilometers driving distance to Mariinskyi Palace and the Verkhovna Rada building, home of the president and parliament, respectively. Luck was on Ukraine's side, though: defending soldiers repelled the attack in time.

The pockets of Russian soldiers elsewhere in the city were in trouble. The intentional design of Russia's offensive meant that they were short on supplies. For the pressure on Ukraine to continue, the Russian convoy would have to link up with them. Consequently, all Ukraine had to do was find a solution to the largest parade of military metal to stroll through Europe in decades.

Embarrassing the Convoy

Unlike the other tasks, Ukraine had a head start on beating the convoy. Before it left Belarus, Belarusian opposition engaged in a rail war, sabotaging train systems and limiting the fast movement of Russian supplies within the country. It was a good first step, but it was not nearly enough to stop Russia. Once the convoy crossed the border, the search for solutions fell to Ukraine. Strategists in Kyiv were up for the challenge, though, exploiting the country's climate and geography to complete the task in front of them.

Satellite photos of Ukraine reveal that the country's natural geography has two halves. The eastern section is defined by wide-open plains, the aforementioned abundant spaces that allow tanks to have free movement. These regions are why Ukraine is known as the "breadbasket of Europe" and beyond. It is also the origin of Ukraine's blue and gold striped flag. The top blue symbolizes a clear sky, while the bottom gold represents a vast grain field.

In contrast, the area stretching from Belarus to Kyiv is heavily wooded. This has critical implications on how to set up ambushes. On the plains, there are few natural places to do so. A defender's best option is to dig a trench and hope to catch the opponent off guard. In the forests, the number of paths is few. Trees line the roads, restricting movement in the same manner that buildings do in an urban setting. Those same trees also provide ample cover and camouflage. Russian troops could drive right up to an ambush point and have no idea what was about to happen until it was too late.

Although described as 64 kilometers long, the convoy was not actually bumper-to-bumper traffic. Instead, it was a series of separate groupings, perhaps a dozen vehicles or fewer at a time, spaced out over that distance. Thus, Ukraine needed to create a strategy to destroy or deter those smaller groups.

The basic playbook that Ukraine eventually settled on is what we might call a "pinch" strategy. Ukrainian soldiers would wait for a set of Russian vehicles to approach a predetermined ambush point. Then, through direct fire, drones, obstacles, or otherwise, Ukraine would immobilize the first and last vehicles in the group. The lead vehicle would often be the easier step because simple barricades—like the aforementioned hedgehogs—could do the trick. The last vehicle required more effort but was vital to complete the task.

Once successfully sprung, Ukraine put all remaining vehicles in a no-win situation. They could not punch forward, either because the first vehicle was disabled or obstacles blocked the path. The point of disabling the last vehicle was to prevent everyone from hitting reverse and leaving the way they came. The final option was to go offroad. In heavily wooded ambush points, this was not feasible at all. Where it appeared to be, Ukraine had an unlikely ally: mud.

Weather was Ukraine's hidden hero. The broader continental region has two rainy seasons: one in spring and one in fall. During these times, *rasputitsa* becomes the bane of everyone's existence. It is a term for the mud that forms on roads as rain washes the surrounding sediment onto the paved areas. With care, a government can mitigate the infrastructure issue by pushing the mud to the side. But it also means that going a meter offroad can be a disaster. Once wheels sink into the mud, it may take a tow truck or even a crane to extract the vehicle.

Ordinarily, *rasputitsa* is not an issue during winter. When the weather gets cold enough, the mud starts turning to ice. Roads simply become slick, not swampy. Slow speeds and appropriate tires allow vehicles to pass without much issue. With that in mind, it is not a coincidence that Russia timed its invasion for the end of February. This was the traditional point of peak freeze—when cold temperatures have persisted for long enough that any leftover water from the fall rainy season has firmed up.

However, there was one slight problem for Russia: the ground never froze. 2022 was unseasonably warm. There were freezing temperatures, but nothing cold enough to transform the mud.

Consequently, once Ukraine immobilized the first and last vehicles in a group, the middle vehicles' only path of escape was to go off road—and pray that the mud would be kind. Executing such a maneuver under normal circumstances would be stressful. Here, though, the drivers had to do it while Ukrainian soldiers were firing at them. Where the mud was unkind, Russian soldiers had to abandon their vehicles and run. This is a major reason why Ukraine recovered so many pieces of otherwise fully functional Russian military equipment. Russia could not simply call for a tow truck or crane with a Ukrainian ambush point right there.

The Irpin River further allowed Ukraine to exploit the mud advantage. It flows roughly north by northeast and runs tangent to the northwestern outskirts of Kyiv, mostly along the inner defense ring. The river then ends at the Kyiv Cistern, an enormous 922 square kilometer reservoir north of the city and part of the Dnipro River.

Ukraine's strategists saw the Irpin as a natural breakpoint, with Russian troops trying to cross it northwest-to-southeast and reach the Kyiv city center. To deny an easy pathway, Ukraine simply blew key bridges that crossed the river. Russia's solution was to construct temporary pontoon bridges. Still, those could require vehicles to go off road. Where Ukraine was lucky, the *rasputitsa* mud locked down the Russian vehicles without further intervention. Failing that, Ukrainian soldiers had another opportunity to shoot at a slow-moving target—artillery loves choke points.

Nevertheless, the height of the mud strategy came when Ukraine intentionally breached the Irpin River dam.

Bizarrely, this caused water to flow back *toward* the river. As strange as that sounds, it was all part of a grand Soviet plan. In the 1960s, as a part of infrastructure upgrades, the Soviet Union constructed the Kyiv Hydroelectric Power Plant. This dammed the Dnipro River at the northern heart of the city. The water that flowed in behind it formed the Kyiv Cistern.

However, the cistern created an issue with the flow of the Irpin River. It fed into the area from the west. But as the reservoir filled, water pooled too far in that direction. Consequently, Soviet engineers had to create a countermeasure to prevent the Irpin River from turning into a floodplain. The solution was *another* dam where the Irpin met the cistern. This compacted the filling area for the cistern into a relatively trimmed canyon. But it also meant that the Irpin River was flowing into a wall. If left unconstrained, the Irpin would create a floodplain all by itself. As such, the dam had water pumps installed that pushed the Irpin's water *up* a few meters to go *into* the reservoir.

When Ukraine breached the dam, that process started to reverse. Water from the cistern receded to the west, expanding the river's width in some areas and causing outright floods in others. Russia's existing pontoon bridges became worthless, the river having become too wide to cross. Places where soldiers previously walked across now needed those bridges. Fringe areas became full-blown mudfests, deterring any tank or other vehicle from approaching. Elsewhere, the mud simply flowed onto the roadways to create a more traditional *rasputitsa* problem.

Even without artificial obstacles, Russia had a hard time staying on the road. Military vehicles are far from lightweight objects. Although an average road can tolerate some level of military-grade abuse, tank after truck after tank after truck is a different story. Once a road breaks sufficiently, the next vehicle is back to traversing dirt. In

Russia's case, vehicles in the convoy returned to a *rasputitsa* situation despite trying to stay on pavement.

The main consequence was the clock continuing to tick. Russia had an optimistic assessment that its troops would reach Kyiv in one day. However, some units took a day just to get out of Belarus because the roads had been torn up so badly. From there, the time bomb began to go off. Vehicles ran out of fuel. Tires started popping. Poorly maintained engines refused to work. Russian soldiers had no idea where their next meal was coming from. And Russia's rigid command structure, combined with a lack of guidance from the beginning, left those soldiers aimless.

By March 11, the convoy had dispersed, no longer in shape to conduct offensive operations. They instead found side roads to hide on, waiting for command to find a solution. But five days later, the roles had reversed. Ukraine went on a counterattack, and Russia had to play defender. The sweep was complete. Kyiv had succeeded in all of its strategic goals. Russian soldiers would not find their way inside the halls of Ukraine's government.

Abandoning the Front

On March 29, a little more than a month after the war began, Russia announced a general intention to leave the Kyiv front and redeploy its forces to the south and to the east. Although the West was skeptical of the declaration, Ukraine indeed retook all of its lost territory in the theater by April 4. In its wake, Ukrainian officials discovered evidence of civilian abuse in the region. The most infamous came to be known as the "Bucha Massacre," occurring in the town just south of Hostomel. The United Nations High Commissioner for Human Rights would later estimate between 73 and 178 civilian deaths. Whatever thoughts Kyiv had about negotiating an end to hostilities elsewhere were immediately erased.

Still, the question of what to do next remained on the minds of Ukrainian strategists. Not all of Ukraine was on the same trajectory as Kyiv. Indeed, the Russian Ministry of Defense framed the entire operation as a "feint" designed to distract the Ukrainian military. By this logic, the Kremlin's true goals were in the south and the east. Distracting Ukraine meant that Russia had a freer hand in the other locations.

However, feints are supposed to be low cost, smoke-and-mirrors operations. The planner sacrifices something small for something else more valuable. Russia's assault on Kyiv did not meet those standards. Rather, a series of strategic, logistical, and bureaucratic blunders prevented Russia from achieving a quick victory in Ukraine. In the process, the Kremlin lost more than time—many soldiers never returned home, and Ukraine expropriated enormous quantities of Russian materiel. Further, crafting multiple plans for Ukrainian presidential succession casts further doubt on the feint framing. Nevertheless, it provided convenient political cover for domestic audiences in Russia. State-controlled media hid the underlying problems, and the average Russian still saw the whole affair as a "special military operation" rather than a war.

Even so, the distraction aspect of it worked to some degree. But that is a story for the next chapter.

The Eastern and Crimean Fronts

Although Kyiv was the focus in international media coverage at the start of the war, Russia initiated attacks on two other fronts on the morning of February 24. Both came from Russian-friendly territory. First, there was the Eastern front. Some of those soldiers descended from Russia proper. Others stormed out of the Donetsk and Luhansk People's Republics, the Russia-sponsored separatist regions dating back to 2014. Second, there was the Crimean front. Almost all of these soldiers came from the peninsula that Russia had annexed eight years earlier.

The stakes on this front may not have been as significant as what was happening around Kyiv, but they would still prove fateful. Had Russia fully succeeded, Ukraine would have become a landlocked country and lost its second and third largest cities. Even with Kyiv still standing, Ukraine would have been stuck choosing between forgoing a large portion of its export business or submitting to the mercy of Moscow. Put differently, these fronts decided whether Ukraine could continue on as a functioning state or would claim the dubious title of a modern-day "sick man" of Europe.

But unlike Kyiv, this story would not have an immediate happy ending for Ukraine. Russia would not be embarrassed on these fronts in the same way. Instead, Moscow's successes would make the war competitive, thereby switching the outlook to a long-term conflict.

Russia's Objectives

Outside of Kyiv, Moscow's ultimate goal was to control what is sometimes called Novorossiya, which translates to New Russia. The territory roughly corresponds to existing administrative borders within Ukraine. Going northeast to southwest, the first layer was the Luhansk, Donetsk, Zaporizhzhia, and Kherson oblasts. The second layer, again going northeast to southwest, consisted of Kharkiv, Dnipropetrovsk, Mykolaiv, and Odesa oblasts. To build Novorossiya, Russia appeared to have had five main objectives. There were three each in what would become the Crimean and Eastern fronts, with one of the objectives overlapping.

The Crimean front originated from the corresponding peninsula, in the southeastern portion of Ukraine. Heading north out of Crimea, Russia had one objective in each of the available ordinal directions. Continuing further north and into the Kherson oblast was the base step as a means of resource control and jumping point for the other two objectives on the front.

Russia's immediate target in this direction was the North Crimean Canal. It flowed—or used to flow—out of this direction. Ukraine's makeshift dam built back in 2014 was an easy target. However, to guarantee long-term control over the water supply, Russia had to travel further north to the city of Nova Kakhovka. This was the sight of a same-named dam and hydroelectric plant that spanned the Dnipro River, which runs east-to-west in the area. Unlike the makeshift canal dam, this one was permanent, an infrastructure project from the Soviet era. The dam created a reservoir to the east. A mere half kilometer upstream was the start of the canal. If Russia could reach that point, then Ukraine would be unable to simply construct another makeshift dam elsewhere on the canal's pathway.

To further secure the area, Russia would want to control Kherson City as well. (This can get confusing. Almost all of Ukraine's oblasts—and indeed all that are pertinent to the story—are named after their capital cities.) It was a population center of just under 300,000 people that indeed served as the capital of the oblast. At 70 kilometers downstream from the Nova Kakhovka Dam, it would be the base of any Ukrainian resistance to Russia's occupation. This was a tricky operation for Russia—Kherson City rests on the opposite side of the Dnipro. But at the same rate, its position made it a potential beachhead for Russia to extend out further.

From there, the Crimean front had two more objectives heading in perpendicular directions. The stretch goal was out west. From Kherson, Russia could drive 70 kilometers northwest to Mykolaiv, the capital of its corresponding oblast. This was a city of 470,000 people but was best known for its shipyards. Indeed, it was closed to Westerners until the 1980s because of its role in constructing the Soviet Navy.

After Mykolaiv would come Odesa, again the capital of its corresponding oblast. The significance of Odesa went beyond that, though—as Ukraine's third largest city, it was affectionately known as the capital of all of southern Ukraine. Its position on the Black Sea and near the mouths of a number of rivers gave Odesa a central position in Ukraine's maritime economy. Reaching it would also seal off Ukraine's access to that end of the Black Sea.

However, in all likelihood, that was not the final stage of the Kremlin's master plan out west. A little further in that direction was Transnistria, a skinny region the runs along Moldova's eastern flank. Decades earlier, the Moldovan Soviet Socialist Republic attempted to break away and become an independent country. The eastern portion of the territory resisted; Moldovans were the ethnic minority there, and many Transnistrians wanted to stay under Moscow's rule. Thus began the Transnistrian War.

Russia's 14th Army intervened, ostensibly as peacekeepers but in practice bolstering the Transnistrian position. The end of the war mirrored what would happen sixteen years later in Georgia with Abkhazia and South Ossetia. Transnistria remained a *de jury* part of Moldova, with only fellow unrecognized entities recognizing its independence. In practice, it was an independent state that relied heavily on Russian protection. Indeed, the 14th Army never left. As such, if Odesa were to fall, then linking to Transnistria would be simple. From there, the Kremlin could consider making it an officially annexed part of Russia.

Heading back to Kherson, Russia's third objective went in the eastern direction. The main prize was Mariupol, with a population of 425,000 and known for its steel industry. This was just outside the *de facto* borders of the Donetsk People's Republic. As a result, Russia's initial work toward this goal would come from the Eastern front.

However, flanking Mariupol by also pushing along the Crimean front was an attractive option. The strip of territory running from Crimea to Donetsk along the Sea of Azov became known as the "Crimean Land Bridge." That is because, as earlier chapters discussed, Crimea was an island from Russia's perspective. Ukraine controlled the only land crossing and was not about to aid Russia's annexation of the peninsula. The actual Crimean Bridge, which spans the Kerch Strait on Crimea's east coast, was its only vehicle crossing. It was better than nothing, but Moscow was still asking a lot from a single piece of infrastructure. Possession of the strip of territory along the Sea of Azov meant control over the highways. In turn, Russia could establish a second method of reaching the peninsula. Combined with a success on the western sub-axis, it would also completely land lock Ukraine.

Along the way, Russia was interested in controlling territory at least up to the Dnipro River, which runs roughly northeast to southwest about halfway up the land bridge. This would provide a natural defensive barrier and reduce some of the complications of controlling such a long frontline. Given that, there were three more assets of high value to take along the way. The Zaporizhzhia Nuclear Power Plant, Europe's largest such facility, was built on the river. It produced 20% of Ukraine's electrical output, and Russia could divert that energy to its preferred locations.

Southwest of Mariupol, Berdiansk was another valuable port along the Sea of Azov that had a series of highways leading to it. Finally, Melitopol was an important crossroads that could serve as a logistical hub, about halfway between the entrance to the Crimean Peninsula and Berdiansk and a little inland.

Heading from the Donbas, Russia had two theater-specific objectives. First was to capture the entirety of the Luhansk and Donetsk oblasts. Although Russia recognized the corresponding people's republics as independent states right before the invasion, neither of them controlled all of the territory they claimed. Luhansk was missing more than half of the oblast, only holding the area around Luhansk City and regions to the south. Likewise, along the other separatist region, a front due south of Donetsk City defined the line of control in one direction. Notably, Mariupol was not within it. Another line heading northeast from the capital formed the remaining border, linking up to the territory that Luhansk controlled. With the recognition of Donetsk and Luhansk a thinly veiled steppingstone to annexation, Russia wanted the complete regions. Moreover, if any areas were going to welcome Russian troops as liberators, these would be them.

Russia's final objective was Kharkiv. The principle here was simple. It was Ukraine's second largest city, with a population of 1,400,000, and the spiritual capital of Eastern Ukraine. Much of that status was a legacy of its time as the capital of Soviet Ukraine between 1919 and 1934. Almost a century later, its political importance continued as the Maidan Revolution unfolded, when Viktor Yanukovych briefly fled there in an attempt to maintain his presidency away from Kyiv. Obviously, that attempt proved unsuccessful. But the Russian language was near-universal there. Had latent support been anywhere close to what Russian intelligence estimated, the invaders would have had a solid base to work from. That, in turn, may have convinced indifferent individuals to fall in line. If so, Russia could have broken the Ukrainian economy in half.

The Southern Front: Initial Russian Successes

To be blunt, Ukraine was not prepared for what was about to unfold on its southern tier. This was due to an accumulation of circumstances discussed in the previous chapters. The bulk of Ukraine's forces sat in the Donbas, both as a legacy of the separatist war and a bet that, if Russia were to invade, Moscow may have only wanted to expand the existing front. When troops poured over the Belarusian border heading to Kyiv, Ukraine had to reassess the situation. That meant drawing troops from the Donbas to protect the capital. In sum, the southern tier was the odd man out.

Thanks to that, when Russian troops departed from Crimea at 4 am, they did not waste any time. Within hours, they captured the makeshift canal dam. Water soon began flowing to the peninsula again. The troops continued north toward the Dnipro River, looking for their next major target.

The other significant gain in the south on the opening day occurred in the northwest end of the Black Sea. In its vast waters sits Snake Island. To describe it as an island is generous. It is mostly inhospitable rock. Indeed, in 2009, Romania and Ukraine took a case to the International Court of Justice to decide whether it was indeed a literal rock or truly an island. Regardless of the label, it had a distinct tactical relevance: unlike the ships patrolling the Black Sea, it was unsinkable. As such, capturing it was an important part of laying siege to Odesa.

At 6 pm, the Moskva, the flagship of Russia's Black Sea Fleet, approached Snake Island. The Moskva dated back to the Soviet era. In fact, it was constructed in Mykolaiv's shipyards under the name Slava, the Russian word for "glory." It had plenty of experience as a veteran of the

Russo-Georgian War of 2008, the annexation of Crimea in 2014, and the Syrian Civil War at various points. Now it was aiming its sights on its original homeland.

Russian soldiers aboard the Moskva radioed Snake Island, demanding Ukraine's surrender. Only 19 soldiers guarded the facilities there, further underscoring Kyiv's lack of preparation in the theater. Moreover, these soldiers were on their own. Since Crimea's annexation, Ukraine had lived with virtually no navy of note. There was no seaborne cavalry on the way to rescue them.

Nevertheless, the Ukrainian soldiers stationed on Snake Island were in no hurry. One picked up the radio and messaged back "Russian warship, go fuck yourself." This would become a meme in Ukraine. The government would later issue a commemorative stamp of the occasion, featuring a Ukrainian soldier giving the finger to the Moskva in the distance. But as much as it became engrained in Ukrainian culture, the verbal barb was no substitute for military might. Russia quickly captured Snake Island and took its caretakers prisoner.

February 25 would see further Russian gains. Having broken the makeshift canal dam the day prior, Russia pushed up to and captured Nova Kakhovka. That granted Moscow control over the main dam that filled the canal and a major bridge that crossed the Dnipro River. It also gave Russian soldiers the opportunity to begin contesting other road and rail bridges to the west that led into Kherson.

Heading east out of Crimea, Russia focused on the Sea of Azov's coastline. Troops initiated a battle over Melitopol, Russia's potential logistics hub. But the real pressure went zooming right past that. On February 26, Russia captured Berdiansk. This was the last major port city along the Sea of Azov before Mariupol. Russian troops were also funneling south from Donetsk in that direction, endangering some of Ukraine's most experienced veterans of the War in Donbas. The only temporary relief Ukraine had was in the coast guard successfully deploying mines along Mariupol's waterfront. If Russia wanted to capture the city, its troops needed to do it the hard way.

Back on the western sub-axis, Ukraine was seeing the first glimmer of hope. Russia was slow to make progress toward capturing Kherson. Perhaps feeling frustrated, Russia tried bypassing the city altogether. The next target in the line would be the shipyards of Mykolaiv. But Russia's strategy there made the same major mistakes as in the Kyiv assault. Only a dozen armored vehicles went on the mission. The gamble was that Mykolaiv's citizens might welcome the contingent, giving Russia a cheap victory and encircling Kherson. Like elsewhere in Ukraine, that assessment was wrong, and the armored vehicles had to turn back.

However, the next three days would produce significant Ukrainian losses. On March 1, it was the fall of Melitopol. On March 2, Kherson buckled from the continuing pressure and fell as well. Mariupol was also surrounded. Ukrainian forces took advantage of the city's heritage and hid out in the vast bunkers of its steel mill. This was another artifact of Soviet-era Cold War planning—steel mills were high value targets, which warranted building otherwise puzzling bunkers. The soldiers withheld their surrender all the way until May 20. But for all intents and purposes, the Sea of Azov was Russia's in less than a week of fighting. Finally, on March 3, Russia captured the Zaporizhzhia Nuclear Power Plant.

The Kremlin's dominoes were falling into place. It appeared that Ukraine might lose its southern tier.

Ukraine Cleans House

Back in Kyiv, the reports coming in from the south drew some serious concerns. The capital was still under imminent danger from the Russian convoy, but the panic of the first few days had subsided by that point. The government's bet that redeploying its defenses westward would invalidate Russia's attack from Belarus proved wise. It also appeared to justify leaving the remaining fronts vulnerable. But the results in the south still raised questions. Ukraine was supposed to see significant losses there, and this was acceptable as just the price to pay for punching Russian troops out of Kyiv. However, the speed and extent of Russia's gains came as a surprise. This was not how the sacrifice strategy was supposed to play out.

The main failure occurred on day one. Despite the absence of forces along the *de facto* border with Crimea, Ukraine was not oblivious to the possibility that Russia could use the peninsula as a staging ground. Over the eight years prior, defensive planners laid a minefield around the area. In fact, the presence of that minefield justified stationing fewer soldiers to the south. Obviously, it could not hold back a Russian invasion forever, nor did Ukraine design it for that purpose. Rather, its goal was to stall an attack for long enough to allow Ukraine to redeploy soldiers as necessary.

However, the minefield failed in this regard. Russia basically ignored the mines and sprinted toward Kherson. That put Ukraine on its back foot. The storming Russian troops were happy to turn the temporary advantage into square kilometers conquered.

Why the minefield failed so spectacularly was unclear. But Kyiv had three theories. First, Russia just got lucky and killed the Ukrainian soldiers responsible for arming the mines before they could complete the task. There was nothing malicious here—luck was just on Russia's side. Second, Russian special forces penetrated the area prior to the attack and disabled the system themselves. This suggested inside help, though special forces plausibly could have done that on their own. Finally, a Ukrainian traitor gave away the minefield's locations or intentionally refused to activate it. Either way, if true, this third possibility represented a disaster for Ukraine.

The Ukrainian Security Service, abbreviated SBU, went on a crackdown. The first step was arresting a Kherson commander, Lieutenant Colonel Ihor Sadokhin, under suspicion that he relayed information about the minefield and helped coordinate Russian air strikes. Zelensky further cleaned house by firing the head of the SBU, Ivan Bakanov. This was less about suspected impropriety and more about ineffectiveness. Bakanov was a long-time ally of Zelensky. They grew up together, and the pair later reunited at Zelensky's production company, before sharing time on the campaign trail. His role at the SBU was to use his entrepreneurial background to root out corruption in the system. With Bakanov apparently having failed, Zelensky moved on.

Ukraine's mistakes went beyond the first day of the invasion and extended to missed opportunities at self-sabotage to slow Russia's advance. Not blowing the bridges leading to Kherson was chief among them. Even though the one at Nova Kakhovka doubled as a critical dam, the broader bridge was independent of the water system. Thus, Ukraine had the ability to prevent Russia from crossing the bridge without causing a humanitarian disaster. This would have come with a number of upsides. First, there would have been no flooding downstream. Second, the canal would have continued receiving water. Finally, and perhaps of greatest importance, the dam maintained the water level to assist in cooling the Zaporizhzhia Nuclear Power Plant further upriver. This is a point that will become important much later.

However, Ukraine was not about to repeat those mistakes. Proactive sabotage was now the order of the day. Any bridges still under Ukraine's control were subject to potential demolition. Meanwhile, Ukraine scuttled the Hetman Sahaidachny, its flagship and the only frigate of its hollowed-out navy. It began the war in Mykolaiv undergoing routine repairs. Although Ukraine had repelled Russia's small test run toward the city, it would not be the last battle there. Moreover, the next strikes would be better organized following Russia's capture of Kherson. Ukraine wanted to deny any chance that Russia might press the Hetman Sahaidachny into service.

Interestingly, while Ukraine was cleaning house, Russian soldiers started looking for houses to shelter, or anywhere else they could find heat and food. Russia's logistical problems on the Kyiv front caught the world's attention, but things were not much better in the south. Russian troops carried few provisions to self-sustain the fight. The miscalculation here was not so much the speed of victory but rather regarding local assistance. The southern and eastern portions of Ukraine had a higher portion of Ukrainian citizens fluent in Russian and with familial ties to Russia. Moscow hoped this would translate into more grateful Ukrainians willing to feed Russian soldiers on their way.

The feed-as-you-go plan largely failed. The cliché that armies march on their stomachs rang true. Without proper meals, Russian troops were slow to advance and became easier targets for Ukrainian defenders. The situation improved once Russia consolidated control over Kherson. Indeed, the infrastructure of the city simplified trying to source provisions locally. However, the issue belied a deeper problem going further to the west.

Ukraine Strikes Back

Kyiv's new strategy limited the operations available to Russia. Having crossed the Dnipro River to reach Kherson, Russia faced a new obstacle. This time it was the Southern Bug River, which flowed roughly north-to-south. Mykolaiv sat on the eastern side, meaning it was readily in play. However, Ukraine could use the river as a natural defensive barrier to inhibit Russia's further progression west toward Odesa. Doing so required blowing the bridges that would otherwise simplify crossing the Southern Bug. Consistent with its new proactive doctrine, Ukraine did not hesitate in that regard.

Russia struggled to find an attractive alternative into Odesa. Earlier on, Ukraine laid a seaborne minefield around Odesa's ports. This prevented Russia from staging an amphibious invasion reminiscent of D-Day's Normandy landings. Thus, Russia's only clear strategy was to capture Mykolaiv. From there, Russian forces could plan a deliberate crossing of the Southern Bug before making a slow plod out to Transnistria.

The key to this plan was Kherson International Airport. Think of it as the southern equivalent of Hostomel, the planned airbridge that was pivotal to Russia's failure in the Kyiv offensive. Despite its international moniker, the airport was small. By comparison, it only accommodated about one percent of the yearly traffic that Boryspil International Airport did near Kyiv. Nonetheless, it was suitable for ferrying in the supplies Russia needed to lay siege to Mykolaiv. And unlike the two airfields that Russia would capture within Mykolaiv, Kherson International Airport was far enough away from the frontlines to safely land planes. However, Ukraine was aware of its strategic importance and gave it the Hostomel treatment. A steady dose of artillery ensured that Kherson International turned into a metallic graveyard. Russia would not have an easy resupply station.

Still, the Russian attack on Mykolaiv marched on. But two more factors kept the city from falling. First, by this point, Ukraine was getting a better sense of Russia's overall invasion plan. As the calendar turned to March, Kyiv was no longer at imminent risk of falling. Consequently, Ukraine could reinforce the southern lines. Second, the earlier betrayals did not persist. To the contrary, Mykolaiv's civilians were calling in the positions of Russian soldiers and facilitating artillery strikes. Mykolaiv was now off the table.

Russia lacked an effective backup plan going forward. One solution was to repeat the bypass strategy. That is, Russia could skip Mykolaiv and hope to find another river crossing further north. Had this been successful, Russian forces could have encircled Mykolaiv. They could then have laid siege to the city or march straight to Odesa. Voznesensk, a small city of 33,000 people that is a 90-kilometer drive from Mykolaiv, became the target. Russia twice attempted to establish a foothold there, once on March 2 and again on March 9. The attacks raised some international concerns because the South Ukraine Nuclear Power Plant is 30 kilometers further north. However, the operations only placed further strain on Russian logistics, and both failed.

With land-based options scratched, Russia's remaining strategy was to invade Odesa from the sea. The Russian Navy would still have to solve the mine puzzle, but success here would have landlocked Ukraine regardless of the outcome in Mykolaiv. To even begin thinking about staging a beach landing, Russia needed to disable Ukraine's artillery out of Odesa. As long as those positions stood, Ukraine could keep Russian ships from approaching the coastline. That meant both minesweepers and landing craft had to stay away.

Nevertheless, true offensive operations to destroy the Russian fleet faced a significant hurdle. Without a navy to engage Russia at sea, Ukraine had to rely on long-distance missile strikes to cause any real damage. But that put Ukraine up against the problem. The Moskva's radar and anti-missile systems shielded the rest of Russia's Black Sea Fleet from any serious consequences. As long as the Moskva remained floating, Russia could continue harassing Odesa. With enough time, the Ukrainian artillery could have failed, and Russian landing parties could have stepped foot in the city.

Instead, Ukraine was the side to achieve a breakthrough. It occurred the night of April 13. A Turkish-supplied Bayraktar TB2 drone loitered in the Moskva's vicinity. What its role was remains ambiguous—it may have distracted the Moskva's crew, provided targeting information to Ukraine, or done nothing at all. Regardless, sometime after 8 pm, Ukraine fired two of its R-360 Neptune missiles at the Moskva. Both snuck past the flagship's defenses and hit their targets. Worse for Russia, the corresponding explosions detonated the Moskva's magazine. The ship began to list to its port side. As the clocks turned past midnight, the Moskva found itself at the bottom of the Black Sea.

Without the Moskva's protection, Russia's remaining fleet pressing Odesa was vulnerable. Moscow made the decision to retreat to the safety of the Sevastopol Naval Base in Crimea. Russia's last remaining option was to use Snake Island as an unsinkable firing position and continue to rain explosions down on Odesa. However, Ukraine relentlessly struck any Russian attempts to set up a functional base there. By June 30, Russia was forced to retreat from the island. Ukraine returned and mounted its flag.

The Battle of the Black Sea was over. Russia succeeded in enveloping the Sea of Azov, but successes around Odesa and Mykolaiv meant that Ukraine would not become a landlocked country.

Meanwhile, in the East…

Russia also found mixed success on the Eastern front. The Battle of Kharkiv must have come as a major disappointment to Moscow. The city would have made a great prize: an enormous population, almost all of whom spoke Russian, and an important legacy from the Soviet era. Its status as the eastern capital of Ukraine meant that it came equipped with roads headed in all directions, which would have allowed Russia to pivot elsewhere. Kharkiv also sat just 30 kilometers south of the border, making it an easy opening target.

The Russian army used Belgorod, a city just inside of Russia, as a staging ground. On the morning of February 24, the soldiers blitzed across and raced to capture Kharkiv. Within a day, they had arrived at the city's edges. But this was Eastern Ukraine, near where war had raged for the eight years prior. Unlike Kyiv, Ukraine was ready for Russian attacks in this direction, even if they were coming from across the border and not from the Donbas. A few Russians breached the city limits on February 27 and 28. However, those soldiers had overextended their supply lines given the number of Ukrainian troops defending the area. Consequently, they had to retreat. The rest of the battle came down to the same problems Russia faced elsewhere: unprepared battalions of soldiers and robust Ukrainian opposition that Russian intelligence failed to predict.

Russia's push toward Kharkiv was short-lived, but its presence around the city was not. For the next two months, Russia would feed Kharkiv a seemingly endless supply of artillery. By the end of it, whatever latent support for Putin's government that may have existed at the start of the war was eradicated. But none of the bombings gave Russia an opening to go into the city once more. By early March, it had become clear that Russia's interests shifted east of Kharkiv, perhaps to link up with soldiers coming from the Donbas.

Speaking of the Donbas, this is where things were going well for Russia, particularly in Luhansk. At the start of the invasion, Russian-sponsored separatist control over the oblast was limited to its southern third, near Luhansk City. That changed almost immediately, with Russian soldiers coming west across the international border. Another salient pointing northwest sprouted out of the corresponding area of separatist-controlled Luhansk. This opened up the opportunity to flank the Ukrainian held land in between. Russia took advantage and collapsed the area, securing control of the vast majority of Luhansk on March 23. On the same day, Russian soldiers pushing out of Luhansk also reached the group that had given up on Kharkiv and instead gone east. Come April, Russia began redeploying soldiers from the failed Kyiv front to the eastern theater. This helped the Kharkiv and Luhansk pushes to fully unite on April 12.

Successes in Donetsk were harder to come by. The aforementioned siege and eventual fall of Mariupol were the highlights. In the process, Russia took full control of the southern portion of Donetsk oblast, securing its coastline along the Sea of Azov. But in terms of territorial capture, much of that work came from soldiers heading north out of the Crimean front. That left close to half of Donetsk—its northwestern portion—still in Ukrainian hands.

The small city of Avdiivka was a microcosm of Russia's frustrations. With a prewar population of 31,000, it sat almost in the center of the oblast—and only a few kilometers away from Donetsk City. Despite being in striking distance of the front lines since 2015, Russian-supported separatists never controlled it. Avdiivka remained obstinate after the invasion began, one part of an apparent wall Russia just could not penetrate.

However, with Russian troops fully filtered into the eastern front, Moscow began claiming more and more gains within the Donbas. They were slow, but they were progressive. For its part, Ukraine pushed Russia further back from Kharkiv and toward the border. Nevertheless, the momentum favored Moscow. Ukraine needed to find a way to strike back, lest Russia eventually consume all of its eastern oblasts.

The West's Slow Response

Ukraine was in the fight of its life—and *for* its life—but it was not alone. The West had no interest in letting Russia break the liberal order it had worked so hard to build since the Cold War ended. Still, the solution to the problem was not simple. The appetite in the West to spill blood was low. This was especially true among European countries closer to the Atlantic, who were both geographically insulated from Russia and lacked the scars of having previously lived within Moscow's sphere of influence. The result was a slow, risk-averse response. But Ukraine eventually began receiving the assistance it needed to survive a longer war against Russia.

A Missed Opportunity

For the United States in particular, two considerations delayed conventional military transfers. Fortunately for Kyiv, the aid turned out to not be strictly necessary for saving the capital. However, the stalled deliveries allowed Russia to penetrate further into Southern and Eastern Ukraine than might have happened otherwise.

The first problem was the shadow of Afghanistan. When President Ashraf Ghani fled the country on August 15, 2021, it did not just signal the end of his government. It also meant the rapid transfer of all government property to the incoming Taliban regime. Unfortunately for President Biden, the United States had spent the last two decades supplying the Afghan government with modern American military hardware.

Had there been a slow, controlled transition between Ghani's regime and the Taliban, the United States would have extracted all of its own equipment or blown up everything it could not have removed. Instead, the Afghan government collapsed in the blink of an eye. The results were images of the Taliban celebrating atop American equipment, some of it brand new. Unsurprisingly, the Biden administration received substantial criticism for having overseen the United States effectively arming its post-September 11 adversary. In that regard, Ukraine seemed like a similar trap. Whatever the U.S. military sent to Ukraine could have soon found itself in the hands of Russia, an American adversary with an even longer history.

The potential negative optics alone did not doom any donation scheme. Rather, it combined with a second point to create the problem. U.S. intelligence inaccurately estimated that Ukraine stood little chance of winning a conventional war. That is why all of the focus on the eve of the conflict was training Ukraine in proper insurgency techniques. From this perspective, whatever might have made it over to Ukraine in time would have had a limited impact. Had the U.S. intelligence community believed that equipping Ukraine would have been pivotal to the outcome of the conventional war, Biden was inclined to make the move. There would have still been some risk in Russia trampling Ukraine and capturing substantial U.S. materiel anyway, but those were the gambles that come with war.

Why the U.S. intelligence community miscalculated here almost as badly as Russia did is unclear. It is possible that much of the assessment was based on intercepted messages coming straight from the highest levels of the Kremlin. Alternatively, the CIA may have had intelligence assets directly within the Kremlin's administration. If so, then Washington would have known the Kremlin's confidence going into the war, and much of the U.S. assessment may have been an extrapolation using that information. The public assessment that Washington was broadcasting indicated that Russia would win but live to regret the consequences of the economic upheaval the West was willing to unleash. That is consistent with the Russian assessment, correcting for Washington having a better understanding that the West planned to resist any annexation of Ukrainian territory.

Regardless, the United States expected Russia to clobber Ukraine. Given that and the concerns about repeating the recent experience in Afghanistan, arms were not immediately forthcoming. This created palpable frustration in Kyiv. Though coalition partners against Russia, Ukraine and the West still did not have perfectly aligned incentives. For Kyiv, any donated equipment or ammunition only had pure upside. For the West, the question was whether a given dollar spent returned at least as much in the form of Russian failure. At the moment, that calculation broke against Ukraine.

There was a small silver lining here, though. For all of the criticism the Biden administration received regarding Afghanistan, first for signaling general American reticence by leaving and then for fumbling the departure, the U.S. military had terminated its longest war in history. Thus, when it came time to pivot to Europe, Ukraine would have Washington's undivided attention. It also meant that the military supplies that the United States had built up in Eastern Europe for Ashraf Ghani were looking for a new home. Ukraine just needed to prove its ability first.

No Go on a No-Fly Zone

When a much stronger actor is about to smash a weaker opponent, the United States has another tool in its arsenal to level the playing field: the no-fly zone. The most recent iteration of that prior to the invasion came during the Libyan Civil War. Almost immediately after organized resistance to Muammar Gaddafi's regime started in 2011, it looked like the conflict was going to end. Although the Libyan Air Force was antiquated, the rebels had no match for it. Without some kind of external intervention, Gaddafi could have picked apart his opposition from the skies and achieved a resounding victory.

However, Gaddafi was a long-time antagonist of the West, and the coordinated rebellion was potentially a one-time opportunity. France and the United Kingdom, along with Lebanon, therefore proposed United Nations Security Council Resolution 1973. Among other things, it called for a no-fly zone over Libya. Ten of the fifteen members of the Security Council voted for it; the remainder abstained.

Two days later, on March 19, 2011, France began imposing the no-fly zone; NATO would later take over responsibilities. With Gaddafi's great advantage canceled out, rebels could safely go on the offensive. Five months later, they captured the capital. Two months after that, Gaddafi was dead.

A strange pairing of hawks and humanitarians pushed for Western states to repeat this course of action in Ukraine. Hawks wanted to take the fight to Russia. Humanitarians wanted to save Ukrainian civilians from the anticipated slaughtering. A Reuters poll on March 4, after about a week of fighting, found that 74% of Americans supported instituting a no-fly zone. It is hard to blame them. The recent history of no-fly zones was full of positive outcomes: the aforementioned Libya case, an extended period in Iraq versus Saddam Hussein, and in 1992 to support Bosnia and Herzegovina. But none of the vocal advocates would get what they thought they wanted. No Western major power seriously considered operating a no-fly zone.

Much of the debate regarding a no-fly zone was misguided. Compared to the 74% of all Americans, only 7% of international relations scholars supported it. The discrepancy arose because many seeking the measure did not fully understand what it entailed. No-fly zones are not simple military operations. Normally, the patrolling country begins by bombing the target country's anti-aircraft installations. That guarantees the safety of the pilots, allowing them to keep their focus on opposing planes. Given that Ukraine would have been a partner country, this seems like a minor issue. Indeed, that may have been true for the interior of the country. But the concerns returned near the border regions, where fighting was the heaviest and anti-aircraft fire from Russian territory was a serious threat.

Thus, option one was to implement a limited no-fly zone away from the main battlespace. Option two was to expand further and bomb Russian installations just past Ukraine's border. Option three was to ignore that step, roll the dice, and gamble that Russia would not risk engaging NATO pilots. No matter the option, though, eventually NATO pilots would have to face the decision about whether to shoot down a Russian plane. Any direct engagement like that with a nuclear power comes with significant escalation risks. When playing a game of nuclear chicken, it pays to put the initiative on the opponent to make the last move before casualties start happening—that is, force the opponent to take the first step toward armageddon. A no-fly zone does the exact opposite. Here, it would have given Russia the ability to challenge the regime without causing NATO casualties. If NATO was unwilling to pull the trigger when push came to shove, then the no-fly zone had no bite, and it was not worth investing the effort to start it.

Then there was a problem with the scope. The no-fly zone over Bosnia and Herzegovina was about the size of Connecticut. Meanwhile, Ukraine is about the size of Texas and a good no-fly zone would have needed full coverage. (This is in contrast to Libya, which is about three times the size of Ukraine but only required patrols over the coastline; the remainder of Libya was strategically unimportant desert for the most part.) Combine that with Russia's more modern opposing air force, and a no-fly zone in Ukraine became a much larger commitment than any of those operations from the recent past.

Finally, the utility of a no-fly zone to Ukraine was questionable. Protecting Libyan rebels, Iraqi Kurds, or Bosnians turned the tides of those conflicts because they were outmatched in the air. Although Russia had the better air force and had accumulated plenty of experience while intervening in the Syrian Civil War, Ukraine never conceded the skies. Russian planes never had open paths to Ukrainian population centers. Ukrainian civilians never endured endless bombing runs. Instead, the main threat to civilians were artillery and missiles. No-fly zones would not help there.

Overall, the combined problems of its unclear utility, the massive scope, and the escalation risks meant that the West needed to look beyond a no-fly zone to assist Ukraine.

The United Nations' Limited Rebuke

Diplomatically, the West struggled to obtain official and meaningful diplomatic sanctioning from the United Nations. As previous chapters have hinted at, the main problem there was the construction of the United Nations Security Council, dating back to its founding in 1945.

International law is a strange world. Unlike domestic legal frameworks, there is no neutral police force that will arrest powerful leaders for violating laws. Instead, enforcement arises on an *ad hoc* basis by countries willing to pay the price and take the risks associated with military action. Nevertheless, insofar as international law matters for coordinating expectations and creating norms, the Security Council is the centerpiece. It is the only arm of the United Nations capable of issuing "binding" resolutions. The meaning behind "binding" here is vague because of the enforcement problem, but it still outranks other international institutions due to that recognized power.

However, the rules of international institutions are a function of the strength of those involved. If such an organization tried to compel a powerful state to go against that state's interests, the state would win that battle the vast majority of the time. Consequently, to avoid descending into irrelevancy, international institutions often operate on two tracks. There are the rules that the powerful states play by, and then there are the rules that the weaker states play by.

From its founding, the United Nations recognized this inherent limitation and built it into the Security Council's formal rules. Today, the Council consists of fifteen members. Ten are nonpermanent and rotate through two-year terms. The remaining five—the United States, the United Kingdom, France, China, and Russia—have permanent membership. They obtained that special status because they (or their predecessor states) were the winners of World War II. That put them in a powerful position, capable of dictating how the post-war world order would work.

But the special privileges continued: they all endowed themselves with veto power. If a resolution has fourteen affirmative votes and one nay, if that nay came from any of the permanent members, then the resolution fails. The permanent members almost always exercise their veto power when unattractive resolutions arise. Only occasionally does one of the veto players get strongarmed into allowing a resolution through despite its reluctance. This occurs when the otherwise vetoing state anticipates that an even worse outcome will arise outside of the system if the resolution fails. For example, China spoke ill of the no-fly zone authorization to protect Libyan rebels. Nevertheless, it abstained from the vote despite the ability to kill the resolution. The reason was that China believed that the West would implement the no-fly zone one way or another, and at least going through the United Nations might restrict its scope. But these cases are rare. Instead, the Security Council caters to the lowest common denominator. This runs contrary to the moral justifications for international law. However, it is the only way to stop powerful countries from flagrantly ignoring the resolutions it passes, which risks the irrelevancy problem.

The result of all of this was that the Security Council engaged in very little effort to rebuke Russia for its invasion of Ukraine. Everyone knew that any attempt to do so would run into the brick wall of a Russian veto. The best they could do was take advantage of some creative workarounds. Veto power does not work on procedural votes. As a result, on February 27, 2022, the Security Council voted to convene a special session of the General Assembly to address the invasion. Russia voted no, but that was not enough to stop it. The subsequent special session, which included all U.N. member states, then passed resolutions that condemned the war and the subsequent humanitarian crisis. But none of these votes were binding. Russia suffered a political black eye, but the rest of the direct consequences were fleeting.

Deploying a Tripwire

That covers the infeasible options and what the United States was unwilling to do. So what was workable? Washington's first step focused on its NATO partners in Europe. As Russia's mobilization increased from January into February 2022, the United States redeployed a couple of thousand troops to Poland and another thousand to Romania. Both countries were NATO members, and both shared substantial borders with Ukraine. The outward appearance was to strengthen NATO's firepower in those regions in case the invasion was a runaway success and Russia further pushed the boundaries.

Nevertheless, the quantity of the forces generated some concerns within the media. Remember, this was a time when most of the world—including U.S. strategists—believed that Russia had a powerful military and that Ukraine would not last long. In that light, a few thousand soldiers seemed like a token force. Obviously, they were not by themselves. Poland alone had more than 300,000 active or reserve soldiers on hand. But adding only 3000 additional soldiers seemed inappropriate given the additional risks that a potential annexation of Ukraine brought.

This criticism missed the strategic goal. The point was not to have those 3000 soldiers survive a battle against a Russian invasion force. Rather, the grim strategy was to intentionally have them die. The prospect that an invasion of Poland or Romania would kill a substantial number of Americans would then deter Russia from trying. If that sounds perverse, it is. But such is the logic of military strategy.

To understand how such "tripwire" campaigns work, it may help to go back to its most famous implementation: West Berlin from the Cold War era. From a defensive standpoint, West Berlin was a nightmare. As World War II drew to a close in Europe, the Western allies and the Soviet Union raced toward Germany. Both sides knew that whoever controlled the land would be in the better position to shape the post-war order. The Soviet Union had a geographic advantage there. Berlin, Nazi Germany's capital and thus its most politically important city, lied in the eastern half of the country. In part due to that, the Red Army arrived there first.

Nonetheless, the Western allies negotiated for partial control of Berlin. The result was a city divided. But the bigger problem was that East Germany entirely surrounded West Berlin. The nearest safe space was 160 kilometers away. Relations between the Eastern and Western Blocs quickly soured, leaving the United States in a quandary: how was it possible to defend a city that the Soviets could attack from all sides and that the West could not resupply?

The answer was that it wasn't. Thus, the question for strategic planners turned from how to win a battle to how to convince the Soviet Union to not even try. This is where the tripwire plan came into focus. Despite the possibility of their inevitable defeat, thousands of U.S. soldiers still resided in and protected West Berlin. In the event of a

Soviet invasion, they could have slowed the attack. However, the strategic realities meant that, in all likelihood, they would have met their end.

Although this would have come as little consolation to those stationed in the enclave, their sacrifices fit Washington's needs just fine. With thousands of U.S. soldiers dead, domestic political fervor would have forced the president to execute a proportional response. In an era of nuclear weapons, though, even measured action risked escalation to the point of annihilation. Working through the consequences, Moscow would have calculated that the risks of taking West Berlin outweighed the reward. But absent the tripwire deployment, the domestic political appetite for a response would not have been as strong. That would have encouraged Moscow to take the risk. Thus, the deployment increased the safety of West Berlin with surprisingly low danger to the potential sacrificial lambs.

Back in the post-Cold War era but before Russia's invasion, the United States executed the tripwire strategy once before in the broader Russo-Ukrainian conflict. After Russia annexed Crimea and launched its shadow war in the Donbas in 2014, NATO's eastern flank grew uneasy. For Estonia and Latvia, this concern was straightforward; both share a land border with the Russian mainland. For Lithuania and Poland, the story is more complicated. They share a border with the Kaliningrad exclave, which Russia kept after the dissolution of the Soviet Union in part due to its warm water port. It remains the home of the Russian Baltic Fleet. Thus, the parallel to Sevastopol was striking—perhaps Russia might consider annexing territory to provide a cushion to a critical naval holding. In any case, Lithuania and Poland share a long border with Belarus, and the possibility of Russia staging an invasion from there was obvious well before 2022.

The United States' solution was Operation Atlantic Resolve. It formalized American troop rotations in those four countries, expanding their numbers to reach a post-Cold War high. This would guarantee that if Russia repeated the Crimea playbook, the tripwire would activate and start a showdown between Washington and Moscow. If Russia went with anonymous "little green men" for such invasions, tying the attack to the Kremlin may have been more challenging. But policymakers in the West knew what was happening at the time—hence the tripwire deployment in the first place. It would not have been difficult to link the two together.

Two years later, NATO formalized this strategy by initiating its Enhanced Forward Presence program. It expanded both the deploying countries and host states. Bulgaria, Hungary, Romania, and Slovakia joined the original four. Each of the eight countries had a "leading state" to bear the bulk of the deployments. As a result, Canada, Czechia, France, Germany, Italy, and the United Kingdom all added tripwires to Eastern Europe. (Hungary was its own "leading state" and thus counts more toward self defense than a tripwire.) Many of the smaller NATO countries, like Albania, Montenegro, and North Macedonia made smaller contributions.

Still, none of this was sufficient for the problem Russia posed as the calendar turned to 2022. With the Kremlin ordering troops into Ukraine, Poland and Romania risked becoming *de facto* border states with Russia. Thus, like Operation Atlantic Resolve before it, those countries appreciated the additional deterrent. But the small deployment had a secondary benefit. A few thousand troops did not constitute a credible invasion force. Moscow could not point to the actions from Washington as particularly escalatory, nor was there any need to engage in preemptive action. In this case, less was more.

The Arms Flow In

The Kremlin expected that the invasion of Ukraine would serve as a *fait accompli*—that the speedy takeover would split NATO and force the West to accept the new Russian order. None of that panned out. Ukraine successfully resisted Russia's initial thrust. Meanwhile, the apparent divisions in NATO regarding the credibility of the Kremlin's invasion plans disappeared once Russian troops crossed the border. A united front emerged in its place.

The aid coalition was large. As the country sounding the original alarm, the United States took an obvious leadership role here. Poland, Estonia, Latvia, and Lithuania committed a disproportionately large amount of aid for their size. However, this makes sense given their geographic positioning and aforementioned strategic concerns. Among NATO countries, they were the most likely next targets for Russia. That being the case, it was better to drain Russian power on Ukrainian soil than on theirs. Norway also ranked high on per-capita aid, perhaps concerned about the small but remote border it shares with Russia in the Arctic Circle. Virtually every other NATO country contributed in some manner. Hungary was the notable exception, with the country having shifted to a more neutral opinion about Russia following Viktor Orbán's return as Prime Minister in 2010.

However, the diversity of the coalition beyond NATO was surprising. Norway's Scandinavian neighbors made a major pivot. Both Finland and Sweden had long histories of neutrality, with Finland's dating back to 1956 and Sweden's dating back to an astonishing 1812. They drifted slightly from that in 1995 by joining the European Union, but the spirit of neutrality continued in both countries. Nevertheless, come the start of the invasion, Finland and Sweden began providing arms to Ukraine. More surprisingly, they applied for NATO membership in May 2022. Austria and Ireland, another two countries noted for their neutrality policies, also supplied Ukraine with weapons. Outside of Europe, Australia, Azerbaijan, Israel, Japan, New Zealand, and South Korea all became relevant contributors.

Still, once the aid began to flow, what Ukraine received was haphazard and insufficient for the task at hand. Part of this was due to long-term apathy, and part was due to lack of preparation for the specific problem Moscow now posed. On the apathy side, many European countries became too comfortable with the post-Cold War environment. It was true that relations had soured with Russia over the previous decade. However, the ideological differences between Moscow and the West in 2022 paled in comparison to the days of Ronald Reagan and Leonid Brezhnev. While the United States continued to spend exorbitant amounts on its military, much of Europe preferred to freeride. Despite an informal NATO goal for member states to spend at least two percent of gross domestic product on defense, few ever met that standard.

Where spending did occur, it was going to the wrong places. The September 11 terrorist attacks marked a shift in Western defense priorities. The days of two large armies squaring off on a battlefield were seemingly over. In its place were asymmetric wars and counterinsurgencies. Defense spending correspondingly shifted to those priorities, with an emphasis on human intelligence gathering and armor against improvised explosive devices. Tanks and massive quantities of artillery were left to rot on the shelf.

As a result, the initial donations Ukraine received were a mishmashed mess, with no coherent central planning. Countries basically went through those rotting shelves, found whatever surplus they had on hand, and sent it over to Kyiv. Austria donated 10,000 helmets. Canada passed along hundreds of thousands of sets of winter gear. Czechia delivered two pontoon bridges. Finland cooked up 70,000 field rations. Ireland provided blood. Luxembourg pitched in by pitching fifteen tents. Slovakia funneled over two million liters of aviation fuel.

Countries also donated plenty of more traditional military aid. MANPADS, the man-portable air defense systems that were key in the Battle of Kyiv, were one of the few transfers made ahead of the war. The flows continued to come in from all over Europe after the fighting began. Javelins were also in high demand, with donations both before and after the start. Recall that these are the weapons with automatic guidance. Specifically, they seek an opposing tank and then arc upward to hit the target at a vulnerable spot. Estonia, France, the United Kingdom, and United States provided some. A variety of multiple launch rocket systems, typically some kind of vehicle with rocket-based artillery, made it over to the battlefield. So too did basic supplies, like rifles, ammunition, mortars, howitzers, and artillery shells.

The howitzers and artillery shells marked an important transition point. Entering the war, Ukraine deployed legacy howitzers from the Soviet Union, which used 152 mm shells. Eastern European coalition partners had some reserve supplies that they could donate, also stemming from their Soviet legacies. However, for new production, they had transitioned to the NATO standard 155 mm. The three-millimeter difference meant that the more ample supplies and production capacity were incompatible with Ukraine's systems. The transfer of American M777 howitzers therefore created new assistance opportunities for other countries.

Ukraine, of course, was happy to take whatever was flowing in. In a scrappy fight, the underdog was not about to bicker with its coalition partners over the corresponding scraps it was receiving. Nevertheless, over the course of a long-term conflict, the smattering of donations was not ideal. Anything beyond a basic weapons system requires some level of training for proper use. Over time, those systems will break down, and their operators will die in combat. When dozens of systems populate the battlefield, Ukrainian commanders cannot simply reassign an alive soldier with a broken weapon to a dead soldier's functional weapon. Likewise, mechanics tasked to repair what broke down could not afford to specialize in particular systems. It was a mess—a product of Western countries choosing to implement stopgap measures, fitting only for the moment at hand.

Nevertheless, on April 25, U.S. Secretary of Defense Lloyd Austin signaled a clear change in policy. Up until that point, the emphasis was on bleeding Russia dry. The strategy paralleled the initial American efforts in Afghanistan in the 1980s, when assistance to the *Mujahideen* intended to maximize pain on the Soviet Union. Eventually, though, the *Mujahideen* showed victory was possible. The United States correspondingly ramped up assistance to give them the tools for the job. Having just returned from Kyiv, Austin announced that the United States would make the same pivot. The West had moved on from Ukrainian survival. Now the task was driving Russia out.

Still, consistent with the concerns about a no-fly zone, Washington was careful to reduce escalation risks with Russia. In particular, the United States did not actually make deliveries to Ukraine. Instead, U.S. shipments would go to the Polish border. Ukrainian trucks would drive across the border, pick up the goods, and then return home. As long as Americans stayed on the Polish side, they received NATO Article 5 protection—that is, the provision in the North Atlantic Treaty that declares an attack on one NATO country is an attack on all NATO countries. Russia was unwilling to challenge that. However, the moment an American went onto Ukrainian soil, Article 5 protection would no longer apply. Washington worried that Russia may have been willing to run the risk under those circumstances and try bombing an American convoy. As such, Ukrainians had to complete the last leg on their own.

As arms deliveries became routine, the next order of business was to implement a long-term plan aimed at removing all the Russian invaders from Ukraine. Despite Ukraine's successes on the Kyiv front, Russia had collected large swaths of territory in the east and the south. Ukraine was not in an immediate position to take any of it back. Russia had learned from some of its earlier missteps and now had time to establish some defensive fortifications. With late fall bringing in another rainy season, it appeared that Ukraine might need to wait until the following year's winter chill to go on the offensive—assuming the ground would ever freeze.

As such, Ukraine sent brigades of soldiers out west, where they would receive modern NATO training. A gamble for the future of Ukraine had begun.

The Economic War

The West may have been slow to provide proper military aid, but the economic war began relatively quickly. After all, this was the plan. Russia would occupy Ukraine, an insurgency would begin, and then the West would attempt to drain Moscow of the funds it needed to continue the battle. The Kremlin shared this same expectation. However, what resulted was a new ballgame thanks to significant Russian miscalculations and an unparalleled response from the world's economic powers. For Russia to survive, the Kremlin needed a well-crafted counterstrategy and fast. Policymakers in Moscow were up to the task, but their temporary solutions built up larger problems for the future.

Fortress Russia

Moscow tried to prepare for the economic war ahead. The annexation of Crimea had taught the Kremlin some important lessons. Any attempt to disrupt the liberal order in Europe might come with a price tag, but it would be denominated in currency and not Western military interventions. As such, the task for Russian strategists over the eight-year period between the annexation attempts was to maximize Russia's economic position while insulating the country from potential sanctions. The policy came to be known as "Fortress Russia."

There is an old joke that Russia is an oil company masquerading as a country. In 2021 alone, Russia exported $55.5 billion in just natural gas, never mind its other energy resources. Much of that income funded traditional government spending. Another chunk went toward Russia's national pension program, something Putin learned not to touch after reforms in 2018 prompted significant protests. But the Kremlin made sure to siphon off a portion of it into a rainy-day fund of sorts, essentially a savings account full of foreign currency and gold. By February 18, 2022, the reserves sat at $643.2 billion.

Once a war started, the Kremlin could draw down from the fund. Wars do not come cheap. Aside from any economic sanctions the West might impose, Moscow also needed to pay its soldiers and produce the metal that those soldiers would use. But whatever pain the West could inflict, Fortress Russia intended to withdraw funds from its savings account to match. Perhaps the West, seeing that Russia could stay afloat for years, would be deterred from implementing serious coercive concessions. In turn, the result could have been a repeat of 2014, where the West sanctioned to express its displeasure but not to the level to force Moscow's capitulation.

However, Russian intelligence's earlier misperception of Western resolve caused another major problem, this time for the Kremlin's budgeting. Of the $643.2 billion in savings, about $300 billion of it sat in Western-controlled accounts. This was a perfectly normal thing to do—money sitting at the U.S. Treasury, European Central Bank, or Japan's Ministry of Finance will not suddenly disappear. But it did mean that the status quo control of that $300 billion was not in the hands of the Kremlin. And soon after Russia invaded Ukraine, those entities froze the accounts.

What looks like an inexplicable blunder in retrospect had a reasonable logic at the time. Those countries enjoyed structural advantages as the pillars of the global economy. But their status as pillars in part came from other countries trusting that they would not exploit some of those advantages—in particular, freezing or expropriating others' assets. After all, doing so made future investors more cautious of placing funds in American holdings instead of, say, Chinese holdings. Locking Russia out of $300 billion of its own fortress would certainly raise those sorts of questions. Thus, the Kremlin wagered that Western countries did not care enough about Ukrainian sovereignty to damage their positions in the global economic order. Consequently, it was not worth the hassle to shift the funds around.

The Kremlin was wrong, continuing in the long line of its miscalculations. The $643.2 billion suddenly grew about $300 billion smaller.

The Sanctions Begin

The West went beyond pressing buttons to lock out Russia from its savings accounts. Traditional economic sanctions came online in a manner unlike anything else before it. Global economic partners had previously shut out other rogue states. Indeed, sanctions regimes against North Korea, Iran, Iraq under Saddam Hussein, and Cuba under Fidel Castro left the target states without functioning economies. But no one had attempted to do something similar to a country the size of Russia.

Not everyone participated in the sanctions regime, of course. India and China were the major holdouts. But the sanctions coalition expanded beyond those providing military aid to Ukraine. Even Switzerland, a country whose neutrality was so strong that it still refused to enter the European Union, and who only became a member of the United Nations in 2002, joined the EU's sanction bloc and froze Russian assets.

Within only a few months, the damage was extensive. $600 billion in foreign capital took flight out of the country, an amount roughly equal to the entire foreign investment in Russia since the fall of the Soviet Union. Not all of that value disappeared overnight. Some corporations chose to wind down operations. Others sold their assets to Russian entities before fleeing—though this latter case left Russian investors with Western businesses but not the Western human capital. Regardless, Russia's gross domestic product entering the war stood at $1.78 trillion. No matter the framing, the Russian economy took a major hit.

With the country locked down, Russians with geographic mobility took the hint. Half a million people left in the war's opening months. For a country with a total population of 144 million, that might seem like a drop in the bucket. However, the type of person departing was not random. Someone who is capable of leaving a country on short notice must have in-depth knowledge of international migration and the means to do it. Once they do so, those people either need to be rich enough that they do not need to work or have skills that facilitate rapid and lucrative employment. In other words, the rich and the most productive workers are the ones who emigrate. They are exactly the type of people you would want in your country if you were about to face economic turmoil. Instead, they stormed out of Russia. Nevertheless, if there was any consolation to Putin, those people were also disproportionately likely to protest the invasion. Russia's economy might have taken a further hit, but the effect on overall regime stability was ambiguous.

The consequences of the West's strategy reverberated through the rest of the world's economy. China may not have participated in the economic sanctions, and its government abstained from voting or protected Russia on many resolutions within the United Nations. However, Chinese companies felt the pressure. Exports to Russia declined from $8.14 billion in December 2021 to $3.8 billion in April 2022. The reason appeared to be fear of something called "secondary" sanctions. These are sanctions imposed on entities doing business with the original sanction regime's target. Here, that meant Chinese companies worried that if they traded with Russia, the West might impose sanctions on them. For many, the choice between Russian markets and Western markets was not close, hence the decline.

All of these effects combined to take a massive toll on Russia's stock exchange, inflation rates, and economic growth. MOEX, the main Russian stock exchange, closed at

3600 on February 16, 2022; on July 29, it closed at 2213. The 39% sell off drew comparisons to the Great Recession, when the United States' markets fell by 56.8%. The key difference was speed. It took 18 months between October 2007 and March 2009 for the U.S. economy to fall that far. For Russia, it was less than five months. Further, those numbers understate the true damage to the Russian economy. Moscow closed the exchanges for a month after sanctions began. When they finally reopened, foreign holdings remained locked. Consequently, the stock prices reflected what Russian investors believed about share values—a group with greater optimism than those who were locked out.

Regarding inflation, Russia entered February 2022 with an annualized 9.2% inflation rate—a number that Western economies would find deeply alarming but was normal for Russia's developing economy. However, due to the economic upheaval, Russian citizens lost faith in their currency and looked to convert it into something physical. Prices soared accordingly. Annualized inflation jumped to 16.7% in March and peaked at 17.9% in April, before tapering off to 17.1% in May and 15.9% in June.

Unsurprisingly, the Russian economy hit a recession. In January 2022, Russia's self-reported annualized GDP growth rate was 5.9%. As the war began in February, it remained at a solid 4.0%. By March, the cracks were showing, as it fell to just 1.5%. April marked the start of the recession with GDP *contracting* by 3.3%. After hitting a 3.9% loss in May, the growth rate bottomed out at -5.1%.

These numbers come with a few important notes. First, the slow dissent reflects how some sanctions cut Russia's ability to import input products for manufacturing, like microchips for vehicle production. Those industries continued production for some amount of time before their stockpiles dried up. Likewise, even when sanctions immediately cut off certain export industries, many companies wanted to draw down their existing supplies for domestic consumption before shutting down.

It is also important to take the numbers with a grain of salt because they were self-reported, and the Russian government had strong incentives to overrepresent the strength of its economy. In that light, the fact that the Russian Ministry of Finance believed it could not plausibly avoid reporting a recession was telling. Facing the unprecedented sanctions regime might seem to imply that a recession was inevitable, but that was not the case. Wars stimulate an enormous amount of government spending. It is possible for the military-induced demand to outstrip the externally-induced losses. This was why World War II helped lift the United States out of the Great Depression. Something similar did not happen here. Still, the increase in government spending offset some of those losses, meaning that the figures were worse than they appeared.

The reason military-induced demand distorts the meaning of GDP figures is that the money has to come from somewhere. For regular GDP growth, the funds come from citizens and foreigners naturally wanting to purchase Russian products. In contrast, anything made for the military comes from the government's coffers. To pay for a surge in arms production and soldiers' wages, the government must raise taxes, borrow money, or dip into savings. From a macroeconomic perspective, raising taxes would have caused a disaster here. During a recession, governments need to stimulate spending. Having higher taxes pulls money out of the economy, causing citizens to be more careful with their rubles. That cure was worse than the disease and thus was off the table.

As a result, Russia projected a 2% budget deficit for 2022. Under normal circumstances, that would not be too concerning. By comparison, the Congressional Budget Office contemporaneously projected a 5.8% budget deficit for the United States. The key difference between Moscow's and Washington's predicaments was access to credit. U.S. bonds are historically some of the world's safest investments, which allows the U.S. government to offer them at very low interest rates. In contrast, the sanctions regime all but cut off Moscow from the international lending market.

The final option was to dip into savings. This was the exact reason Russia had started building its fortress eight years earlier. But within five months, Russia had already burned through $75 billion of it, in addition to the $300 billion frozen.

The Kremlin's Short-Term Crisis

In times of war, economic sanctions raise two immediate concerns within the halls of government. First is the country's ability to fight the conflict effectively. This was a minor issue for the Kremlin during the opening phase of the war. Russia had sizable existing stockpiles of weapons and ammunition. Moreover, it was an arms exporter. Many of those defense industries would eventually run into production problems, but that was an issue down the road.

Instead, the main immediate concern preoccupying the Kremlin's time was regime stability. The economy was not going to completely collapse overnight. But it was clear to the average Russian that the country was approaching a fiscal cliff. No matter how much value someone placed on the annexation of Ukrainian territory, the economic sanctions tied to Russia's invasion were obviously responsible. If the economic tumult turned into a catastrophe, the Kremlin could have started facing active resistance at home. That would have meant either an end to the war or great risk to the regime's survival.

Within the first few days, Russia faced a banking and currency crisis. Russian citizens could see that the ruble was about to lose substantial value. Under such circumstances, the best way to respond is by converting that currency into something—anything—else. Foreign currency or durable goods would do. But the preliminary step for any of that is for citizens to access their money.

Thus began a bank run. Even on a normal day, the average bank is in a precarious position. When clients deposit money, bankers do not simply leave all of it sitting in a backroom. They need to make money to pay their staff, cover rent, and turn a profit. As such, banks act as complicated macroeconomic middlemen for depositors and those wishing to take out loans for businesses, mortgages, or whatever else. However, there is a significant asymmetry between the agreements with depositors and with those receiving the loan. Depositors can remove their money at any time. Loans, in contrast, have an agreed upon time horizon. In turn, banks cannot hope to pay back all of their depositors if everyone shows up at the same time to close their accounts.

The problem goes so deep that bad expectations can instantly dig an otherwise healthy bank into the ground. Under normal circumstances, there is unanimous agreement among depositors that allowing the bank to continue its operations normally is the best outcome for everyone. Indeed, if you know that everyone else will only make standard withdrawals, then your best strategy is to do the same. Moreover, everyone else may feel the same way. This is why banks operate without issue the vast majority of the time.

However, if you hear that everyone else is trying to withdraw all of their funds immediately, your best move changes completely. Suppose you continue life as normal. Then, by tomorrow, all of the other customers will have pulled their money from the bank. But the bank does not have the liquidity to pay everyone. As a result, the bank becomes insolvent. You live to regret your decision to continue as normal, as now the bank cannot repay its debt to you.

The insidious part is that this thinking is contagious. If each individual believes that everyone else will pull their money tomorrow, then each individual ought to rush to the bank. But that justifies the common expectation that everyone plans to close their accounts. This self-fulfilling prophecy aspect of the problem is why a bank with perfectly healthy fundamentals can still face a bank run. Add a very real and very public crisis—say, an invasion of your neighbor and the imposition of massive economic sanctions—and all you are doing is stoking the flames. Even if financial experts in the Kremlin knew that the sanctions could not cause any systemic issues on their own, that might not have mattered. If everyone thought that others thought that disaster was on the horizon, the self-fulfilling prophecy would have kicked in anyway.

Under ordinary circumstances, the modern solution to bank runs is something known as deposit insurance. The majority of countries have some program like this. In the United States, the Federal Deposit Insurance Corporation (FDIC) manages it. In Russia, the responsible party is the Deposit Insurance Agency. The basic premise is that the insurer will pay depositors the value of their accounts (up to some limit) should their bank become insolvent. The beauty of the system is insurance often solves the problem that would otherwise require the insurance. Even if someone suspects that their bank is about to collapse, there is no need to run to make a withdrawal. The government will cover it shortly after a failure. As a result, few people sprint to the bank at all. The bank remains solvent, and the insurance agency does not ultimately need to make any payments.

Unfortunately for the Kremlin, Russia's economic woes were on a scale that deposit insurance could not solve. The problem for the average Russian citizen was with the ruble itself. If a bank failed, given the rest of the chaos in the country at that moment, depositors would have needed to wait a long time for the government to make them whole.

In the meanwhile, the purchasing power of their deposits would have plummeted. The situation was worse for depositors with accounts denominated in foreign currency, as they would have needed to wait and see how the Ministry of Finance would have converted those lost funds. The end result saw Russian banks with lines out of the door—proof that average Russians were aware of the scope of the problems the war had caused. The near-universal bank run threatened to crash Russia's economy even before Ukraine could push the invaders out of Kyiv.

International currency exchange markets reflected the problem. On February 14, 2022, 100 rubles bought \$1.30. For the next four weeks, the ruble entered freefall. By March 10, 100 rubles purchased just \$0.74.

Consequently, the Russian Central Bank needed an alternative solution. The answer was interest rates. On February 28, the Central Bank hiked the rate from 9.5% to 20.0%. This did not directly protect Russians from insolvent banks. It did, however, change individual calculations. There was now a greater reward for keeping money in interest-bearing accounts. Furthermore, the move was public, so everyone knew that everyone else was aware of it. Thus, it also alleviated the meta-problem by convincing people that others would be less inclined to continue the bank runs.

Beyond that, the Kremlin made a few other key interventions to preserve the ruble's value, at least on the surface. First, it slowed ruble trading. Russian citizens could no longer use formal means to make foreign money transfers. Daily rubles exchanged plummeted by 80% as a result. Domestic lending was restricted to rubles, which some lenders had avoided previously due to the currency's instability. Russia's exporters—at that point, the energy companies still finding markets for their products—had to convert 80% of their reserves into rubles. Thus, the Russian government was buying dollars and euros while forcing demand for rubles, at least in-country. The end result was that official exchange rates on July 31 were 100 rubles for $1.61, somehow $0.31 *more* than before the war started.

That said, not all was what it seemed. The Russian Central Bank had accomplished the herculean task of propping up the Russian economy. But all of these steps were trading immediate problems for future problems. The official exchange rates were meaningless, an artifact of what the Russian government said rather than what black market exchanges reflected. Higher interest rates ended the bank run. However, few self-respecting businesses were about to invest in new projects when interest rates were surging. Russia was already facing a recession. The standard macroeconomic solution under such circumstances is to cut interest rates, stimulate investment, and build back economic growth. The Central Bank was forced to take the opposite path in regard to interest rates—an even worse recession was still better than complete economic insolvency. Besides, the military-induced demand would pick up some of the slack created by private investment cratering.

All told, the Russian economy was not going to self-destruct. If Ukraine were going to win the war by default, something else had to give.

Popular Uprisings, Coups, and Coordination

Though Russians were not about to go hungry in the streets, the economic damage wrought on the country was immense. Further, within a few days of the invasion's initiation, the world realized that Russia would not trample over Ukraine; within a month, it became clear that any gains would be limited to the country's eastern half and come at a high price. Combined, from the outside, the Kremlin appeared at risk of regime change.

Putin undoubtedly felt greater pressure in March 2022 than just two months earlier, but the danger to the Kremlin was not as bad as it seemed. Broadly, regime change could have come in two different forms: popular uprisings and coups. Organizers for either method faced significant coordination problems. Putin exploited these to insulate his regime in relative safety given the circumstances.

First, consider a popular uprising. The central challenge for autocratic regimes more generally is that a country's population always vastly outnumbers security forces. On any given day, if the entire population of a country made a concerted effort to remove top-level leadership, they would succeed. The problem is that doing so requires collective action. If one person shows up on a street corner by himself, he is an easy mark for security forces. At best, he might spend a night in jail. At worst, he may never see his family again.

However, there is safety in numbers. If the entire city comes out to protest, now the security forces are in trouble. An attempt to repress the protestors could backfire, as the masses vastly outnumber those loyal to the state. This is why autocratic governments work so hard to stop protests before they start. China's internet censors, for example, are willing to tolerate some level of criticism of the government. But any suggestion that citizens engage in collective action to voice their displeasure is subject to speedy deletion.

Overall, the incentive structure has a similar flavor as the bank run problem from earlier. Two separate expectations are self-reinforcing. If no one expects anyone to come out to protest, then no one individual wants to alter their plans. After all, it would be a bad idea to stand on the street corner by oneself. However, if each person expects everyone to march on the streets, then the logic of safety in numbers kicks in. Some risk-averse individuals may still wish to stay at home. But many enjoy being actively involved in revolutionary social movements. If they know that their participation will not result in their inevitable arrest, then they prefer taking part.

This is why autocratic governments can suddenly come to a rapid end. Two examples from the end of the Cold War are striking. On December 21, 1989, long-time Romanian leader Nicolae Ceausescu staged a rally in Bucharest. The ostensible purpose was to demonstrate the regime's strength in the shadow of some protests away from the capital. A few screams and jeers among the 100,000 plus in attendance snowballed. A momentary lull allowed Ceausescu to finish his speech. But after it ended, the rally turned into a protest, the protest turned into a riot, and the riot turned into a revolution. Four days later, Ceausescu was executed.

The precise moment of the fall of the Berlin Wall was even more bizarre. By November 1989, the East German government had made substantial reforms, but the state itself did not appear in imminent danger. One of those reforms was to allow for limited, regulated travel into West Berlin. On November 9, government spokesperson Günter Schabowski drew the job to announce the new regulations. However, he had not received a full briefing on the policy. As a result, when asked when the new policy would go into effect, he guessed "without delay."

That was not what the government had planned. Border guards had yet to be briefed about the new policy. But the average East German citizen was unaware of the confusion. They simply congregated around the Berlin Wall's gates, as Schabowski had suggested was legal. West German broadcasters captured video of the growing crowds, which carried over into the East German airwaves. With people seeing that they would not be alone, the crowds only ballooned from there. Border guards, confused about what was happening and vastly outnumbered, simply conceded and let everyone through. Thanks to the safety in numbers and Schabowski's accidental coordination, the Wall fell.

In contrast to Romanian and East German leadership, Putin had one key thing going for him at the start of the invasion: he was genuinely popular at home. In the wake of the successful and largely costless annexation of Crimea, Putin's approval numbers peaked at 88%. Attempts to address pension reform cooled those numbers to the mid-60s in the second half of 2018, where they remained other than a minor dip at the peak of the COVID-19 pandemic.

Of course, public polling in autocratic countries is always a dicey affair. Some respondents may fear that the government is listening in and will punish them if they voice displeasure. Fortunately, political scientists have methods to indirectly estimate approval. In an experimental survey, respondents can be randomly divided into two groups. One receives a list of various political leaders, and the respondents are asked the total number of individuals from that list that they support. The second group receives an identical list but with an extra name added to it—here, it would be Putin's. Again, they are asked for the total number of individuals they support. Thus, at no point is anyone directly declaring their feelings for Putin.

Nevertheless, the researcher can take the second group's average number of leaders supported and subtract that by the first group's average number of leaders supported. The difference is the estimated implicit approval rating of Putin from the second group. That is because the groups are the same in expectation and the surveys are identical except for the extra name. Thus, whatever difference arises between the two must either be attributable to that additional name or random noise.

In 2015, researchers Timothy Frye, Scott Gehlbach, Kyle Marquardt, and Ora John Reuter commissioned this exact experiment. Putin's popularity remained high even when using the indirect method. To answer their title question "Is Putin's Popularity Real?": it appeared so, or at least it *was* so before the start of the invasion.

Why Putin was popular is another story. The Kremlin's control over the media narrative certainly contributed. But part of it was a fundamental shift in Russia's status going from the Soviet era, to the Yeltsin administration, to Putin's ascension. For all its fundamental flaws, the Soviet Union turned a failing imperial empire into one of the world's two superpowers. The economic crisis precipitating the Soviet Union's dissolution and Yeltsin's subsequent mismanagement of the transition caused a status deficit. Putin's rise—buoyed by rising energy prices—led to Russia's reemergence on the world stage. The average Russian citizen viewed him as a reformer. Whatever problems existed in Russia were not Putin's fault. Rather, Putin was in office trying to resolve all of the problems in front of them.

Regardless of the source of Putin's popularity, in terms of trying to deter a mass uprising, this was a good place to start. If few individuals want to remove you from office, then security forces have fewer potential hotspots to track. But the perception of Putin's popularity was almost as important as the reality. It was possible that the standard surveys were wrong, and that Russians were so reticent that they still included Putin on the approved list even when not directly asked about him. However, that was not what the average Russian thought, and the Kremlin-controlled media was not about to dispel that perception. Given that, trying to start a protest movement seemed like a losing proposition. Other political opponents shared that expectation, meaning they were also doubtful that more would show. Whatever Putin's true popularity was, the coordinated expectation was to not protest, and that was a self-fulfilling prophecy.

That left the possibility of a coup. The motivation may have been there. Displacing an autocrat and securing power for yourself is a ticket to riches and a place in the history books—*if* the coup is successful and *if* you can hold onto power in the following days. Some within the Kremlin may have also believed that the invasion was a bad policy decision and thus a seamless coup was in the Russian state's best interest. Some within the FSB in particular appeared to prefer continuing covert, subversive means in Ukraine even if the intelligence suggested that a traditional war could work.

However, Putin's popularity put potential coup organizers behind the 8 ball. The start of the invasion brought Putin a 'rally round the flag effect, surging his approval rating—if opinion polls were still to be believed in a time of crisis. A successful coup plotter would have to somehow convince the masses that their support for Putin was misguided, lest the plotter face a popular uprising. This was essentially the problem that doomed the 2016 coup in Turkey—President Recep Tayyip Erdoğan was popular among Turkish citizens, which prevented the plotters from reaching the necessary critical mass.

The logistics of a coup created another obstacle. Like popular uprisings, coups are another exercise in coordination. In any regime, some portion of the political power players are staunch, genuine advocates for the leader. Some portion secretly seek change. But the bulk are interested in their own survival and continued political career. The coup plotter's goal is to convince each person in this middle group that everyone else has already switched allegiances. At that point, resisting the coup plot is futile. Thus, everyone in the middle group must play an awkward guessing game. If they all bet that the coup plot will be successful, then it *will* be successful by virtue of the coordinated change in allegiance. But if they all bet that it will fail, then the plot is hopeless.

Putin's careful control over top political appointments meant that any plotter would have to meet a hefty burden of proof. For example, suppose elements of the FSB started claiming that everyone within the Kremlin supported a coup. Then military intelligence might have become confused. What exactly happened to cause so many Putin loyalists to sour on their long-time leader? The FSB could have spun a good story, perhaps based on estimates of the economic damage Russia would suffer by continuing to fight. But it would have needed to be extremely compelling before anyone bought it.

One final hurdle coup plotters faced was another product of Putin's popularity. The more genuine support exists for a leader, the less the state needs to empower security forces to counteract subversive behavior. This is good news for the leader. The more powerful individual security forces are, the easier it is to do the grunt work of coup plotting—securing government buildings, taking over media channels, closing key roads, and so forth. Putin had already gone into the standard coup-proofing handbook and hedged against this by dividing security services among many organizations. But the fact still stood that he could keep the services relatively small—especially by Soviet standards. That meant he could more effectively screen who was coming in and then monitor the organizations as time progressed. All of these factors would have led to greater skepticism about a coup plotter's alleged support.

Russia's Long-Term Arms Crisis

Although the sanctions bloc did not pose imminent danger to Putin's regime, the Kremlin still faced long-term issues with the war. Part of this was keeping the production lines of the Russian war machine humming. Militaries do not begin wars with everything that they need to achieve total victory. Maintaining the necessary stockpiles to do that during peacetime is simply way too expensive. Instead, think of pre-existing armaments as startup funds. They are there to tide over the military until the government can spool up the assembly lines.

Though Russia kept its latent military capacity in better shape than Europe, this was still an opportunity for the West to exploit. Modern weapons of war are not the simple machines that Kalashnikov rifles once were. Fighting vehicles can have tens of thousands of individual parts.

Some of these are non-negotiable—if engines do not work, chassis break down, or wheels immediately pop, then there is little point in producing the vehicle at all.

If a country manufactured all of those input goods domestically, economic sanctions would not be much of an issue. The government might feel some economic constraints on paying the suppliers, but the sourcing is never in question. However, that is not how post-Cold War economies work. Certain components require significant specialization to produce, never mind to do so efficiently. The result is that defense production has globalized—not to the same extent as the civilian sector, but the evolution is notable.

Within large alliances like NATO, this has been a fantastic development—member states can dependably rely on one another and exploit the efficiency gains without worry. But problems arise when companies source components from unfriendly countries, as was the case with Russia. Once sanctions came down, any Russian manufacturer that relied on Western imports was eventually going to run out of supplies. How long before the assembly lines ground to a halt depended on how much of the components the manufacturers had in storage.

Russia had some creative solutions available to delay that outcome. The government could cannibalize other systems with the key components and then supply them to the manufacturers. The only real long-term solution, though, was import substitution—that is, to begin producing the goods at home. Ironically, Russia received short-term boosts from North Korea and Iran precisely because long-running sanctions regimes had forced them to already master import substitution. But neither country could produce at the level that Russia required. Instead, Russian businesses were in a race against the clock to bridge the gap that Western countries had left behind.

The centerpiece of this problem for Russia was semiconductors. On a technical level, a semiconductor is a material that conducts electricity, but not fully. Hence the name. On a practical level, they are a necessary component for devices that convert electricity to processing power. As a result, just about every piece of modern technology is crawling with them—including Russian drones, tanks, and planes. Even basic bullets and artillery shells come from manufacturing equipment that runs on semiconductors.

Unfortunately for the Kremlin, semiconductors are incredibly difficult to produce and did not play to Russia's comparative advantage in the world economy. Moreover, the country accounted for less than 0.1% of the world's semiconductor purchases. As such, there was not much demand for domestic semiconductor manufacturing. Russia tried despite those hurdles, in part due to Fortress Russia security policy. However, many of the manufacturers went bankrupt. Those that survived were small and produced low-quality chips. They also ran into a problem further emblematic of the situation: the Russian companies relied on Western components to produce the semiconductors. Thus, they could not continue production once imported materials ran out until Russia found a way to self-manufacture those as well.

As a result, semiconductor sanctions took a heavy toll on Russian output. In the years prior to the war, Germany was Russia's leading chip exporter, and the United States ranked third. Those options ended with the start of the war. To fill in that demand, Taiwan was a sensible place to look. The island was the dominant power player in the industry, producing 60% of all semiconductors and 90% of the most advanced ones. But Taiwan joined the sanctions regime as well.

The next best solution appeared to be China, previously Russia's second largest chip exporter. Nevertheless, this was not a quick fix. Semiconductor manufacturing slowed during the COVID-19 pandemic due to supply chain issues. Despite that, demand surged. Even in February 2022, the issues persisted on both sides. As a result, China did not have spare manufacturing capacity to pick up the slack.

Still, China helped Russia through a process called "parallel importing"—using an unauthorized intermediary to purchase a banned product. Here, that might have meant China buying chips from Taiwan and then selling them to Russia. Sanctions regimes are not naïve to this type of workaround. Removing a product from any marketplace opens up new profit incentives. If someone can buy for the global price and quickly turn around to sell at a black-market premium, middlemen are going to line up immediately. Even Turkey, a NATO country, took advantage. The task for sanctions regimes instead is to make this process as frustrating as possible for the target and raise the price paid to cause additional burdens. In that light, they are more like taxes than outright bans.

Indeed, despite their best efforts, parallel importing could not satisfy the Russian war machine's chip hunger. Ukraine reported recovering Russian military equipment with semiconductors from dishwashers and refrigerators. Russia apparently had scrapped the consumer devices to feed the military's semiconductor needs.

Russia's Long-Term Financial Woes

Resolving all of the issues with Russian arms production required a great deal of money. That was where the second long-term problem with economic sanctions took effect. The purpose of any general trade embargo is to shrink the coffers of the target government. When wars become industrialized battles of will, the country that cannot or will not pay the price to continue fighting ultimately loses. Failing that, the opposing ruler may succumb to a domestic uprising or may have to leave the war to stop that from happening. Either way, the sanctioning states win.

Regarding Russia, not everything was on the table for the West. Attempting to shut down Russia's grain and fertilizer industry would have caused too many secondary problems. Russia was the world's largest exporter of wheat and the fertilizer used to grow that and other products elsewhere. The West was eager to level the Russian economy, but not at the cost of domestic turbulence in the Middle East and North Africa. Indeed, those regions imported a large portion of Russian grain. But regardless of the destination, dwindling global supplies would have disproportionately caused trouble there. Grain is fungible—consumers do not care about their grain's origin so long as they get their calories. Thus, had Europe's imports suddenly disappeared, its grain consumption would not have simply ended. Instead, being the wealthy countries that they are, they would have just paid the higher price to import from elsewhere. Poorer countries—like those in the Middle East and North Africa—could not have matched those prices. Consequently, they would have gone hungry.

Europe knew this all too well. Prior food supply crises led to immigration problems for the continent. A repeat of that would risk fracturing the sanctions regime. Targeting food production was therefore counterproductive if the West wanted to sustain long-term economic coercion against Russia.

To make matters worse, Ukraine was the world's fifth largest wheat exporter. Most of its shipments came from Odesa and surrounding ports. They went into the Black Sea, through the Bosporus Strait, and along the Mediterranean. Ukraine's own sea mines, meant to deter an amphibious Russian landing, also stood in the way. Once in the Black Sea, Russia was still trying to impose a blockade. All told, no one was interested in loading grain onto ships and sending them on their way. Rail infrastructure could not pick up the slack either, in part because Ukraine's lines ran on the old Soviet standard gauge, making its train cars incompatible with European partners.

The solution to these problems became known as the Black Sea Grain Initiative. Technically, they were two separate agreements, with both warring parties individually partnering with Turkey and the United Nations. Russia allowed Ukrainian grain transports to traverse the Black Sea unimpeded. Turkey, acting as a neutral party, facilitated inspection of ships going to and from the Bosporus Strait to ensure that no forbidden materials passed through. In return, Russia secured access to worldwide markets for its food and fertilizer exports. This was less about the actual movement of goods and more toward giving Russia's financial system the ability to process that trade.

Outside of the grain industry, the West had two significant structural advantages, both connected to Russia's oil industry. The first was simple: Russia's economy was not built for efficiency. Like many autocratic countries, oligarchs dominated Russian industries due to their connections with the government. That is the point of an extractive regime. Growing the overall economy is not the goal. Instead, the game for the ruling regime becomes how to keep as much for themselves as possible. Under such circumstances, the market does not select winners based on their economic productivity. Rather, those who better master corruption take over large swaths of the economy.

Even extremely autocratic regimes still face a binding constraint here. If they capture too much for themselves, they risk inciting a popular uprising. During boom periods, meeting the broader population's minimum demands is simple. In Russia's case, this was a matter of energy prices. When oil and gas commanded a premium, Russia became rich. When prices plunged, turmoil triumphed, as the last of the Soviet commissars knew all too well. International conflict tends to drive energy prices up. But if the West could convince everyone to refuse Russian exports, the rest of the economy would be a mess of inefficient industry.

The second structural advantage was more complicated. Russia had an underlying problem that economists call "Dutch disease." The term originates from a phenomenon the Netherlands experienced after discovering enormous natural gas deposits in 1959. Despite its silly name, Dutch disease has serious economic consequences.

Consider an economy with three sectors. First is natural resource extraction: oil, gold, or diamonds as examples. Second is manufacturing: production of cars, heavy machinery, or computers. Third is services: fancy restaurants, theme parks, or sporting events. Each is humming along in balance with one another.

Then one day the country discovers enormous gas deposits right as the world experiences a surge in energy prices. This is the favorable position Russia found itself in after the turn of the millennium. Cash was plentiful, allowing Putin to ride a surge of economic growth and erase the Russian malaise of the Yeltsin years. It also led to the surpluses that built the $643.2 billion fortress Russia rainy day fund. This was a boon, and the Kremlin did not hesitate to exploit it. And despite the trouble that would come later, the average Russian would happily repeat it.

However, without careful management, an imbalance arises. Due to changes in labor and exchange rates, not all domestic industries benefit from the resource boom. When extraction accelerates, that sector needs to hire more workers. For the oil and gas industry, this effect is small because they are not especially labor intensive. However, the wealth created within the sector is enormous. The newly enriched people will want to use their money to have some fun. The country's service industry becomes an indirect winner. But now all of the caviar bars and massage houses need to hire to meet demand. Labor within the country becomes constrained.

Businesses in the manufacturing sector start to worry. The labor constraint forces them to increase wages to recruit and retain employees. Failure to do so means that flexible workers will shift to the service sector. That makes the manufacturers less competitive on the international market. Some will have no choice but to close up shop.

Worse, the new energy exports cause the local currency to rise in value. Foreign buyers want to purchase the oil and gas. In Russia, the simplest way to do this is to buy the products in rubles. But that increases ruble demand and thus increases its price. Even sales denominated in foreign currency have the same effect. Russians who want to purchase services in Russia need rubles to do so, and thus still need to make the conversion. However, the higher value of the ruble makes it cheaper to buy imported manufactured goods. More of the uncompetitive domestic manufacturers now have to abandon their businesses. The end result is a strengthened economy overall but at the cost of gutting the manufacturing sector.

Although domestic winners and losers are inevitable in a world of free trade, Dutch disease comes with an additional risk. Imagine that energy prices were to suddenly fall off a cliff. Russia had experienced this multiple times before, whether due to U.S. fracking increasing supply, Saudi Arabia turning on the spigot for the same effect, or a pandemic cratering demand. Obviously, this creates a problem for the Russian energy sector. But the spillover effects cause further pain. The service sector relies on customers coming in from the energy sector. Meanwhile, the manufacturing sector cannot pick up the slack in the short term. It has already been gutted, and investors are going to be cautious before rebuilding the infrastructure that could turn unprofitable when energy prices rebound.

Critical for the war effort, Dutch disease also meant that Russia was vulnerable to economic sanctions. If the West suddenly stopped importing Russian oil and gas, then the energy sector would evaporate. The ramifications would be enormous. In 2021, Russian exports were worth $492 billion, $212 billion of which came from the energy sector. Without those funds, the service sector would also likely evaporate. That would then put an enormous burden on manufacturing to pick up the slack—a seemingly impossible task without access to international markets.

Indeed, the West pushed in this direction at the beginning of the war. The United States and Canada banned Russian energy imports almost as soon as the first Russian crossed Ukraine's border. This was easy to do because, given the geography, neither country depended on Russia for energy. Europe also had broad support for an oil ban. The petrol market was already globalized, so Europe could just replace Russian exports with a more expensive alternative from elsewhere. However, natural gas in Europe was a sticking point. With the bulk of Russian exports heading in that direction, inaction there would have completely undermined the effectiveness of the sanctions regime.

The crux of the problem was transportation. Natural gas was critical to heating systems and industrial production throughout the continent. Nevertheless, transporting gas is difficult. The simplest solution is pipelines. The exporter can pressurize the gas on site, pump it into a pipe, and quickly send it to the end user. Pipelines are expensive to build, but once in operation, the per unit cost of transport is a bargain. As a result, Russia has a number of pipelines running into Europe. One even went through Ukraine and continued to process 43 million cubic meters of gas daily even during the war. Ukraine did not mind taking part in this apparent absurdity because its own transit fee made up for what Russia was earning.

In the past, pipelines were the only commercially viable method to transport natural gas. If pipelines were infeasible or no end user was nearby, oil companies would flare the natural gas on site as a waste product. Fortunately, the commercialization of liquified natural gas, or LNG, provided a solution. At room temperature, the energy density of natural gas is low. Putting it into a tank and then transporting the tank to the end user is not economically viable. To solve that problem, the LNG process supercools the gas to -162 degrees Celsius, turning it into a denser liquid. That allows enormous quantities of gas to travel across the world at relatively low prices. In turn, LNG created a globalized market for natural gas. It also coincided with the U.S. fracking boom—LNG allowed American exports to reach Europe for the first time at scale.

There were still two barriers that stopped Europe from breaking free of Russia's energy grip. First, pipelines remained the more efficient method of transit. Second, the global market for LNG relies on countries installing terminals at their seaports. Terminals convert the liquid back into a gas and place it into a pipeline or the local infrastructure. This meant that landlocked European countries that relied more on the traditional pipeline method could not easily make the change.

Western allies were more frustrated with Germany's position. With a sizable coastline, Germany could have invested in LNG terminals like many of its European neighbors did in the two decades prior. Instead, Berlin chose to engage with Russia. This led to the creation of the Nord Stream pipeline, running from gas fields near Saint Petersburg, through the Gulf of Finland, and into the Baltic Sea before arriving in Germany. As an earlier chapter touched on, construction of a second pipeline began in 2011, only pausing briefly following the annexation of Crimea. By 2021, it was waiting to come online pending final regulatory approval from the German government.

The plan backfired, and Germany found itself funding the Russian war machine. The solution was to finally build LNG terminals. Even by racing to do so—relaxing all sorts of regulations in the process and delaying the planned shutdown of nuclear reactors in the interim—the first one would not open until December 2022. In the meantime, Germany had to stock up on its gas reserves. This created a period when demand for Russian gas soared. Coupled with higher prices globally due to the geopolitical instability, Russia raked in the rubles. Any attempt to exploit Russia's Dutch disease had to wait.

Russia took the opportunity to find new export partners. Turkey was an attractive option given its proximate location, but it could not absorb everything Russia had in surplus. The real solutions were China and India, with a combined population of around 2.8 billion people. But geography and capacity were the tradeoffs. Oil tankers only took two days to reach Eastern Europe, four days to reach Northern Europe, and seven days to reach Western Europe. In contrast, it took 27 days to go to Southeast Asia and 35 days to go to East Asia.

There was also a satiation point. Existing businesses were happy to take a discount on Russian oil, but they were fully cognizant that this was a windfall from the war. As soon as the sanctions ended, their prices would go back toward pre-war levels. As such, few businesses were willing to invest in new infrastructure. Instead, they maximized production with what they had on hand. Some of the oil wound up back on the international market under a new flag, with the middlemen capturing the price difference. Even Saudi Arabia—one of the world's largest oil producers—began importing Russian oil for that purpose. In sum, Russia could not substitute all of European demand in Asia, and what did make it out of the country needed to sell at a lower price to entice customers.

The result was a substantial discount on Russian oil. Consider a barrel of Urals oil, the benchmark for a Russian oil mix coming from the Ural and Volga regions. Prior to the war, it usually traded just below Brent crude, the European benchmark originating from the North Sea. By July 2022, the difference became a yawning gap—Brent sold for $110 a barrel, while Urals only commanded $82. The decreased demand and social stigma for Russian products was having a significant effect.

But sanctions alone would not be enough to end the war on favorable terms for Ukraine. Rather, Kyiv also needed to start producing results on the battlefield. And they were about to arrive faster than just about anyone anticipated.

The Kharkiv Counteroffensive

Back in Kyiv, military planners faced a dilemma in how to structure the next phase of the war. After a successful first phase of defending against the initial invasion, a lull fell over the battlefront. Russia had made significant gains in the east and the south, but the rhythm of the war was beginning to shift to a stalemate. For Ukraine, this was far from a satisfactory outcome. Russia held the majority of territory of the oblasts along the Crimean land bridge and held small swaths of a couple more. With Western support funneling in, Kyiv believed it could do better than that.

However, as alluded to earlier, Ukraine faced two countervailing incentives. The summer months were ticking away. Come late fall, rains would pour down once again, limiting Ukraine's ability to conduct offensive operations. That could have pushed the stalemate all the way to the spring of 2023. Russia would have used that time to fortify its positions and raise the cost of any Ukrainian counteroffensive. On the other hand, Ukraine had sent many of its most promising troops to the West for deeper training. Waiting until 2023 meant bringing a more professionalized army into the fight.

At the time, most analysts suspected that Ukraine would play the slow game, unable to formulate an effective plan with its status quo holdings. That, in turn, raised fears that Western audiences would grow frustrated with Ukraine's lack of progress. If borne out, Kyiv might have seen its assistance disappear, and then no long-term offensive would have been possible.

Ukraine proved those analysts' first expectation wrong. Kyiv had a plan that would leave the Russian army in chaos and the Kremlin scrambling to find a solution.

Choosing a Target

Conditional on not waiting until the following year, Ukraine's first order of business was to establish a target for a prospective counteroffensive. There were two straightforward options: Kherson City and the outskirts of Kharkiv.

When Russia stormed out of Crimea and turned west, the invading soldiers' failure to capture Mykolaiv created an obvious strategic vulnerability. Moscow ordered the crossing of the Dnipro River, anticipating that troops would reach Odesa and form a defensible front along the coastline. Instead, Russia failed to pass the Southern Bug River and retreated. This created an isolated pocket. Going upstream along the Dnipro, Russia controlled territory many kilometers past the river, going all the way until it curved near the Zaporizhzhia Nuclear Power Plant. Russian command could still resupply the local units via bridges over the Dnipro, but it was a dangerous place to be. An offensive there would have also allowed Ukraine to recapture one if its oblast capitals, even if the majority of Kherson oblast lay on the river's opposite side.

The other option would again take advantage of an earlier Russian failure. In the first few days of fighting, Ukraine beat back the invasion force at Kharkiv. Months of artillery fire did not change that, but Russia still held a strip of territory north of the city along the international border. Further, Russia controlled smaller towns and cities to the northeast. That mattered due to Russia using Belgorod as its logistical hub for operations in the north. Because Belgorod is north of Kharkiv, controlling those outlying areas was necessary to keep a clean flow of supplies heading into the Donbas. Success there would liberate some Ukrainians, but the main advantage was strategic—it would put Kyiv in a better position for further offensives later. In contrast, liberating Kherson would put Ukrainian troops up against the Dnipro River, making any follow-on assaults unlikely.

Despite the limited opportunities in the south, Ukraine believed that Kherson—and its population of 279,000 people—was the bigger priority. It also appeared vulnerable enough that Ukraine could make a play for it without having to wait for Western-trained troops. Ukraine quietly began shaping operations in the middle of July and made some small gains along the frontline northeast of Kherson. However, further advances failed to make progress. By August, Russia went back on the offensive in the area and picked up new territory to offset the losses. It appeared that Ukraine's counteroffensive had stalled before it even started in earnest.

Ukraine's partners in the West also grew concerned. Running the numbers, Western military analysts warned Ukraine that continuing along that vector was a waste of resources. Despite the Dnipro creating a bottleneck, Russia was still funneling too many supplies and too many troops into Kherson. With battalions of Ukrainian soldiers away to train for 2023, Kyiv could not muster enough to overcome Russia's entrenchment. Ukraine needed a new plan. Otherwise, it would be a long wait until spring.

Putin's Political Handcuffs

Ironically, Russia's successes along the Crimean and Eastern fronts created a critical vulnerability for the invaders. It was the same problem that doomed the Kyiv offensive and the attempt to stretch to Odesa: a lack of manpower. 200,000 soldiers sounded like enough when half of Ukraine was going to welcome its liberators and pledge allegiance to Moscow. It was not enough to capture Kyiv when Ukrainians offered active resistance. And after the Kremlin learned its lesson and redeployed its Kyiv battalions to the east, the influx of troops was barely enough to scrap together the new land Russia controlled.

Defending that territory brought new challenges. The frontlines stretched 1300 kilometers. The good news for

Russia was that transitioning to the defense meant that it benefited from fighting behind fortifications. The bad news was that Ukraine could choose where along the frontline to attack. If there were one weak point along those 1300 kilometers and Kyiv could find it, then Ukrainian soldiers could push right through the entrenchments. They could then turn to the left and right, flanking Russia and rendering the other fortifications ineffective.

Under ordinary circumstances, an invading government might look at the situation and do *something*. A hypothetical Russian withdrawal from the invasion zone might have been an overreaction—the contemporary problem was a strategic deficiency, not necessarily a sign of an inevitable defeat. But maintaining the status quo was playing with fire. To secure the new holdings, the invading government needed to raise a larger army.

But this was Russia, and Putin did not yet have the resolve to go that far. The invasion remained a "special military operation." To call for a general mobilization would shatter that illusion. Moreover, Kherson was still an occupied territory. It would take extra juggling to conscript soldiers and then ship them to Ukraine. Putin's political interests did not yet align with the Russian state's interest. If there was still a chance Russian forces could hold the frontlines as they were, he preferred to maintain the status quo.

Enter HIMARS

Putin's handcuffs gave Ukraine an opening. And planners in Kyiv were receiving a new tool that would change the course of the war: the High Mobility Artillery Rocket System, or simply HIMARS. The broader public was unaware of HIMARS before the war began. In part, this was because the system was relatively new. But it did not take long for it to become common among those following the conflict to recognize it as an integral part of the battle space.

The origins of HIMARS date back to the end of the Cold War. During the superpower conflict, the United States was preparing for a long, drawn-out slugfest with the Soviet Union. One of the key tools in the American arsenal was the Multiple Launch Rocket System, or MLRS. At first glance, it looked a bit like a tank: wide, sturdy, and equipped with tracks to move through a combat environment. However, its back half can rise up at a 45-degree angle to reveal a hidden rocket system. For long-range artillery fire, it was the go-to option.

Nonetheless, as the Cold War drew to a close, the Department of Defense speculated that the future of U.S. conflicts would center around short, rapid deployments. In that regard, the MLRS was lacking. It was clunky and required enormous—and therefore expensive—C-5 planes as transports. Essentially, given the predicted future of warfare, the U.S. army demanded a sleeker, downsized version of the MLRS. The Gulf War further validated this belief. As a result, HIMARS received the full green light.

The first HIMARS tests began just months later. Rather than make the system look like a tank, the principle of simplicity demanded that a regular truck serve as the base. But even a weapons system that planned to borrow much from MLRS designs still took time to do research and development on. A truck that can fire rockets was a simple idea, but in practice having a chassis capable of withstanding the thrust was a challenge. Lockheed Martin received the main contract for prototypes in 1996, with the army and marines receiving evaluation models in 2001 and 2003, respectively. That pushed the bulk of operational deployment past the start dates of U.S. major combat operations in Afghanistan and Iraq. The conflicts the United States participated in since then did not capture the public's attention to the same extent as the invasion of Ukraine, hence HIMARS' anonymity.

Famous name or not, HIMARS was an invaluable tool. One major problem that traditional artillery has is heft. Unlike small arms fire, artillery launches light up their operators like a Christmas tree. That goes double for large rocket systems like what both MLRS and HIMARS used. This is concerning because opposing artillery has an opportunity to fire back. HIMARS has two defenses against this. The first is range. Washington had earmarked a large supply of Guided Multiple Launch Rocket System rockets for Ukraine. Abbreviated GMLRS (pronounced "GIM-lers"), these rockets have an 80-kilometer range. Only extreme opposing artillery can return fire at that distance.

However, MLRS can also fire GMLRS and doubles HIMARS' capacity, with twelve rockets versus six. What makes HIMARS unique on the battlefield is its mobility. It not only looks like a truck, it also acts like a truck. Slimming down the width and replacing the tracks with regular wheels trimmed HIMARS' weight to 16,250 kilograms fully loaded compared to MLRS' 24,040 kilograms. The wheels meant that HIMARS needed roads to effectively maneuver. But assuming there was a place to drive, its operators could fire their rockets and then sprint out of there at 85 kilometers per hour.

Even better for Ukraine, the truck-based design made it easy to deliver to combat zones. All it took was a workhorse C-130 plane, a driver to bring it aboard, a pilot to fly it to the recipient country, and another driver to take it off the plane and head to the firing site.

Washington gave Ukraine only one restriction: do not use HIMARS to attack Russian soil. This, again, was about managing escalation risks between Russia and NATO countries. The White House did not want to give the impression that it had any desire to pursue a conflict past the 2014 borders. Depending on where Ukraine fired GMLRS missiles, the 80-kilometer range could easily breach that policy. However, doing so would endanger future

American resupplies. For that reason, the U.S. military did not transfer Army Tactical Missile System rockets to Ukraine. Abbreviated ATACMS, they are also compatible with HIMARS launchers. The key difference is range—ATACMS go up to 300 kilometers. The White House believed that such an option would be unnecessary given the restriction, though some parts of the land bridge remained outside of GMLRS range.

Minding the U.S.-imposed limits, Ukraine's first order of business was to begin attacking Russian supply depots along the Crimean land bridge. Wise defenders place such depots far away from the frontlines. Doing otherwise makes them easy targets for traditional artillery. Worse, if the offense overruns the defense's positions, then suddenly all of that metal switches hands. Thus, Russia placed theirs further back, say between 20 and 50 kilometers, looking for the right tradeoff between safety and faster delivery times.

This was step one of Ukraine's HIMARS strategy. Russia was not prepared for the HIMARS deliveries. Ukraine therefore found no shortage of supply depots to blast with GMLRS rockets. After the fireworks displays racked up, Russia's local commanders got the idea and implemented two immediate countermeasures. First, for supplies that had to stay close to the frontlines, Russia decentralized the operations. Ukraine could still hit the smaller depots, but the supply of GMLRS was not endless, and a single successful hit would no longer completely handicap the area's operations. Second, for the remaining supplies, Russia pulled back the major stockpiles behind the 80-kilometer radius and therefore outside GMLRS range. Still, Ukraine indirectly benefited from the response due to the longer Russian supply lines and delayed replenishment to Russian soldiers under the gun.

With the juicy targets gone, Ukraine moved to step two of the HIMARS strategy. If Kyiv could no longer have its soldiers hit the targets, then they would strike the infrastructure instead.

A Bridge (or Three) Too Far

Ukraine had all of the ingredients for a successful counterattack: a steady supply of HIMARS, 1300 kilometers of frontline to manipulate, and an insufficient number of enemy soldiers defending those lines. However, the military needed to revise its original plan to take back Kherson. Going straight for the jugular was a bad idea. Instead, the solution was to initiate a drawn-out siege of the city, force Russia to commit troops there, lock them into place, and then aim the thrust of the attack elsewhere. Only afterward could Kherson come back into focus.

The key to all of this remained Kherson's perilous geographic position. On the opposite side of the river from the rest of Russian forces, resupply into the city relied on three bridges—infrastructure that Ukrainian troops had failed to dismantle during their retreat in the opening days of the war. The most direct route was the Antonivsky Bridge. Named after the Kherson suburb it went to, the bridge spanned the Dnipro River less than 10 kilometers upstream. It was a part of the larger E97 highway that started in Kherson, went to Crimea, crossed the Crimean Bridge, and continued running along the Black Sea clockwise, hitting Russia, Georgia, and Turkey. Given that status, it could handle significant traffic.

The second was the Antonivsky Rail Bridge. It was about six kilometers further upstream and served a different purpose. Russia preferred to ship much of its military supplies by rail. A single train could carry dozens of tanks along with ammunition and personnel. All of this could travel by traditional vehicle roads, of course. But the efficiency gains were substantial. More importantly, all tanks and armored personnel vehicles can only travel a limited number of kilometers before they should go in for maintenance. Ideally, Russia wanted to limit those kilometers to actual combat situations and not transport. There was also the weight problem previously experienced in the Kyiv offensive. Paved roads are not meant to support the burden of all that armor. As columns drive over them, eventually the roads will give way. In contrast, rails are designed to withstand the corresponding pressure. As a result, the Antonivsky Rail Bridge was a valuable asset for Russia.

The final crossing was the Nova Kakhovka Dam, previously noted for its versatility as an electrical power plant and basis for the North Crimean Canal and the Zaporizhzhia Nuclear Power Plant's cooling systems. But it had yet another role, with both a vehicle and rail bridge sitting on top of the dam. The downside was that the bridge sat much further upstream from Kherson along the Dnipro. Still, a 72-kilometer drive was better than nothing.

Fortunately for Ukraine, all three bridges sat within HIMARS range. Artillery crews therefore spent July and August hammering them. For the first two near Antonivsky, this was straightforward. Bridges of that size are sturdy by design, and GMLRS rockets are not large enough to break them under ordinary circumstances. But that was not the point—and in some ways ran contrary to Ukraine's goals. Instead, the aim was to make them impassible. Sinking the bridges was unnecessary and would cause further headaches to Ukraine following a successful counteroffensive in the region. A few holes in the road or rail were sufficient. Their proximity to the city came with another benefit. Whenever Ukraine hit one, an endless supply of social media posts with images of the bridge would follow. Planners back in Kyiv had all the open-source intelligence they needed to correct any mistakes.

The bridge along the Kakhovka Dam required a little more finesse. The dam itself was sturdy—mere artillery fire would not be enough to cause a catastrophic breach. But chipping away at it did not sound like an attractive option either. Fortunately, another benefit of the GMLRS system is accuracy. Ukraine believed that it could strike the road without hitting the dam. HIMARS units therefore went to work, causing the same transportation problems as downstream.

By the middle of the summer, Russia had no easy path into Kherson. It was a never-ending cycle: Ukraine would puncture holes in the pathways, Russia would try to patch them, only for Ukraine to make new holes. Eventually, Russia tried setting up pontoon bridges nearby, but Ukraine received intelligence on those and struck them all the same. It was still possible to move soldiers and materiel in and out of the city. But what mattered for Ukraine was that the process took forever.

Springing the Trap

Wars are guessing games. The offense wants to anticipate where the defense is entrenching and go to the opposite location, where resistance will be minimal. The defense has the exact opposite incentives. When intelligence is poor, the best either side can do is act unpredictably, preventing the other from adopting the appropriate counterstrategy. This is why countries go to great lengths to deceive the other side. For example, in 1943, British intelligence launched Operation Mincemeat. The plan involved dressing an already-deceased body in a major's outfit and giving him fake messages about an upcoming invasion of Greece. The reward was Nazi Germany diverting resources to there and leaving Sicily poorly guarded for the true attack.

Unfortunately for fans of international intrigue, the days of such grand deception may be over. The upshot for Ukraine was that the planners back in Kyiv knew exactly where Russian troops were going—U.S. spy satellite imagery gave away all the relevant information. Though Russia also benefited from observing Ukraine's movement, that did not matter much. The steady dose of HIMARS attacks had rearranged the chessboard in Kyiv's favor. Despite the transparency of the Ukrainian plan, Russia now faced a dilemma. There were no good solutions, only the lesser of two evils.

Distance and broken bridges set the scene. If Russia wanted to protect Kherson, it needed to pre-position ample resources there. If Russia failed to do so, Ukraine could have rushed the city, used the river as a de facto rear flank, and encircled the troops. At that point, Russian soldiers would have either needed to surrender *en masse* or would have faced total annihilation. Overprotecting the city to keep Ukrainian forces further back was the only viable solution. However, that left Russian forces near Kharkiv understaffed and the area ripe for the taking.

Of course, Russia could have chosen to reinforce its northern positions. That would have deterred Ukraine from striking in that region. But then Kherson, the original target of Ukraine's counteroffensive, would have been defenseless. Russia could protect one, not both.

Half measures were even worse ideas. Under normal circumstances, positioning the bulk of Russian forces in between Kherson and Kharkiv might have seemed like the appropriate response. Moscow could have waited until Ukraine committed to one of the vectors and then dispatched the reinforcements to the appropriate location. However, there were two issues with that. First, it risked Ukraine applying pressure both north and south, delaying the true commitment and taking advantage of the short-staffed frontlines. Second, Ukraine had the mobility advantage. Its equipment was in better shape, its supply lines were shorter, and most of the infrastructure west of the frontlines remained intact. HIMARS rockets were not just targeting the bridges near Kherson. They were also hitting roads and rails running up and down Russia's supply lines.

Dividing the troops seemed like a bigger recipe for disaster. Ukraine then could have responded by concentrating its forces in one area and run over Russian positions there. The Russian troops on the opposite side of the 1300-kilometer front line and the three bridges would not have had time to help. Then Ukraine could have redeployed and repeated that process in the other position.

In short, the Kremlin had to pick one place to save. Kherson won out—presumably because its status as an oblast capital made it the more valuable of the two prizes. The Russian military managed to sufficiently resolve its Dnipro River problem and provided Kherson with enough supplies and men to deter an attack. Ukraine needed to head north to Kharkiv.

Rout in Kharkiv

For careful observers of Ukraine's quiet summer counteroffensive, the wait was frustrating. Two months of probing near Kherson showed few net gains. Without a broader view of the war, it was easy to conclude that Ukraine had made a massive mistake and should have held back until its troops completed Western training.

Almost overnight, public opinion completely flipped. Russia did not want to abandon its positions around Kharkiv, so its soldiers stayed put. But they would soon be running for their lives. On September 6, Ukraine began its counteroffensive in the north. With Russian positions understaffed, Ukraine advanced at a blistering pace. Tanks raced toward their targets without forewarning, forcing Russians to abandon their positions within seconds. Ukraine once again recovered an abundance of Russian equipment.

Meanwhile, the scrambling Russian soldiers retreated to locations still ill-prepared to stop the assault. Traditional artillery had softened up the original frontlines, but Ukraine had also positioned HIMARS around Kharkiv to strike deeper Russian positions. Thus began a virtuous cycle for Kyiv, where the first attack would create chaos in a second position, attacking the second position created further chaos in a third, and so forth. The initial results were so promising that the goal shifted. Rather than only remove Russia from the Kharkiv oblast, it became possible to push into Luhansk and Donetsk and further disrupt Russian supply hubs in Ukrainian territory.

Within four days, the counteroffensive was already a resounding success. Ukraine had already reached Izium, home of a key railway station. The following day, Russia announced its intention to withdraw to the Oskil River, which runs roughly north to south just inside of Kharkiv oblast. In theory, that should have given Russian troops a more defensible position that might have stemmed the bleeding. However, Ukraine was already approaching the river from all directions. 48 hours later, Ukrainian troops crossed the Oskil to set up bridgeheads.

Still, the distance covered was beginning to take its toll on Ukraine's offensive. In some places, troops had traversed 70 kilometers. They were not yet exhausted, but the fuel gauges were running low. Soldiers simply cannot continue their battle mindset indefinitely without declining in their abilities. Equipment also needed routine maintenance. The abundant stockpiles of ammunition and artillery necessary for an offensive push were dwindling. Over the next couple of weeks, Ukraine moved back into Luhansk and maintained pressure in Donetsk. Ukraine's final major gain came on October 1 with the capture of Lyman, another railway hub.

By the end, Ukraine reasserted control of over 12,000 square kilometers, or about seven percent of its lost territory. The West now had proof that Ukrainians not only could defend against Russian attacks—they could actively emerge victorious in offensive operations.

The Kherson Counteroffensive

With the offensive in Kharkiv winding down, it appeared that Ukraine had made its major impact for the year. Time, territory, and troop transfers were now all working against Kyiv. Summer had literally run out. Moving from September to October brought a ticking clock. Rain would soon start falling. At that point, Ukraine could no longer match its signature speed from Kharkiv. Meanwhile, the further Russia pulled back, the shorter the frontlines became. Retreating eastward also contracted Russian supply lines, eventually reducing the chaos of the retreat up north. Worse, Kherson was the next plausible target for Ukraine. But Russia had just sacrificed all that territory in the north to lock up the south. It once again appeared as though Ukraine might need to hold back until its Western-trained reinforcements arrived.

Ukraine's prospects were about to take another hit. Russia's disaster in Kharkiv served as a wakeup call for the Kremlin. The political chains were about to come unleashed. And yet, through further careful planning, Ukraine would secure the original goal of its summer counteroffensive within a couple of months.

A Special Military Operation No More

Russian hardliners were displeased with how the retreat from Kharkiv unfolded. From their perspective, Putin was soft. He did not want to risk political turbulence at home, so he started the war with a modest mobilization. When that proved insufficient to take Kyiv, Putin redeployed those troops to the east. But it was still painfully clear that those troops were unlikely to hold the gains Russia made in the opening weeks of the invasion. The Kremlin needed to take decisive action to prevent a larger catastrophe.

Putin granted those hardliners their wish on September 21. Broadcasting on national television from his office,

Putin gave an address reminiscent of the original invasion announcement. The contents matched the earlier tone as well, though further dialed up. What started as a "special military operation" had become a war against the West as a whole, under the guise of the Ukrainian regime. The initial deployments were insufficient to deal with the threat, and so Russia needed to undergo a more general mobilization.

The speech marked a point of no return. Putin could have used the opportunity to declare mission accomplished in Ukraine and bring home the troops. Within Russia, the political narrative at that point remained one of a limited engagement with correspondingly limited casualties. By this logic, Ukraine had a Nazi problem and was collaborating with the West to militarize against Russian interests. Over the six-month operation, Russia had eliminated the Nazis and destroyed untold amounts of Ukrainian military equipment. The task was over. Ukraine had learned its lesson, and so Russia had no further business in the country. Or so that could have been the Kremlin's rhetoric.

Such a retreat would have undoubtedly infuriated the hardliners. It would also have been implausible to Russians who better understood the dynamics of the conflict. However, Putin still controlled the media. With sufficient spin, there was a good chance that enough people would have accepted that narrative, and Putin could have continued in office. But that was not the path he took. Whether he worried about a hardliner coup or believed that the narrative would fail may never be known. Regardless of the reason, the speech made it *his* war. Putin would have to deal with the long-term consequences, good or bad. His term in office would be intertwined with the outcome, even if failure still did not guarantee his departure.

Within the speech itself, details surrounding the mobilization were scant. The text of the official mobilization decree offered little help. A follow up speech by Minister of Defense Sergei Shoigu appeared to reveal the first clues regarding the scope: 300,000 troops would be conscripted to staff the frontlines and prevent a repeat of the Kharkiv counteroffensive.

Many doubted those figures, from potential draftees to Western observers. A study titled "Married and Drafted" by Mediazona, a Russian opposition media outlet, indeed indicated that this was a significant understatement. It analyzed marriage rates inside of Russia before and after the mobilization. Ordinarily, marriage licenses required a one-month waiting period. However, conscripted soldiers received an exemption and could get married on the same day. This was because only officially married spouses received death benefits in the event that the husband died in war. Thus, conscription provided a strong push for any couples previously on the fence on whether to marry.

Because of the different time horizons between standard marriages and conscription exemptions, any sudden spike immediately after September 21 in marriages could only have come from the latter group. This gave the researchers an estimate of the excess marriages that mobilization induced. They then took that information and compared it to census data on individuals cohabitating with their partners—that is, the pool who might file for a spontaneous marriage. Combining those pieces of information together created an estimate of the percentage of all such individuals who received draft notices, which could then be projected to the entire population of eligible men. The final estimate? 492,000 people, more than 60% greater than what Shoigu advertised. Bribery and medical disqualifications may have ultimately reduced that number, but it still stood much higher than the public declarations.

The reaction among the mobile Russian populace was unsurprising. Previously, Russia saw an exodus of individuals who were hurt by the economic sanctions. Now, just about all military-age men were on the hook. Those who knew of the realities in Ukraine and had the ability to leave tried doing just that. A source within the Kremlin claimed that the FSB counted 261,000 men departing over the first five days following Putin's speech. Border crossings in Georgia, Kazakhstan, and Belarus filled up with bumper-to-bumper traffic. One-way plane tickets on the international routes still flying were sold out. In the strangest case, two men floated a small boat along the Bering Strait. They requested asylum upon hitting Alaska.

Those without the means to travel took advantage of a bizarre aspect of Russian mobilization law. To be officially called to service, the draftee needed to physically receive the summons. If the draft board could not locate an individual, then he remained free. Thus, many sought refuge in vacation homes or friends' or grandparents' homes, hoping to ride out the storm.

Not everyone was equally at risk. The data on excess marriage rates showed great geographic variation. Moscow and Saint Petersburg had among the most total men drafted. But when adjusting for their status as the two largest cities in the country, they were among the *lowest* in percentage of eligible men drafted. Instead, the eastern regions were overrepresented. It appeared that draft offices attempted to minimize the political blowback of the new policy by targeting the politically unimportant regions.

There was still the matter of sending conscripted soldiers abroad, a tricky question in Russian law. In parallel, the Kremlin had a plan for that. The overall strategy mirrored the proceedings in Crimea eight years earlier. Russia would sponsor a referendum with the areas regarding annexation. International monitors would note that the elections were neither free nor fair. Returns would show overwhelming support. Then the Kremlin would host a ceremony welcoming the new territory to the federation.

Luhansk, Donetsk, Zaporizhzhia, and Kherson were not as simple. Although the results from the Crimean referendum were tainted, Western polling firms found that a majority of Crimeans believed that the more popular alternative won. Resistance in Zaporizhzhia and Kherson was stronger. Meanwhile, despite eight years of investment in separatist movements, the Luhansk and Donetsk People's Republics never drew oblast-wide support.

The war itself added further complications. The Kremlin appeared to want to sponsor referenda earlier in the invasion. However, failures along the Kyiv front created doubts about whether Russia's gains in the east would hold. November became the new target time. But then the Kharkiv counteroffensive created new urgency and a demand to send conscripted soldiers into the regions.

Thus, Russia held four separate referenda, one for each oblast, from September 23 to September 27. For Luhansk and Donetsk, the question asked whether the respective People's Republic should be incorporated into the Russian Federation. Zaporizhzhia and Kherson had similar wording, removing the People's Republic language and adding phrasing for the oblasts exiting Ukraine. The official tallies showed the vast majority of voters in each region in favor of their respective referenda. Luhansk and Donetsk led the way, with each seeing more than 98% of votes in favor. Kherson dragged up the rear, with "only" 87% support.

The elections received heavy international scrutiny. The United Nations special session passed a resolution condemning the referenda as illegal. Only five countries voted against it: Russia, Belarus, North Korea, Syria, and Nicaragua. China notably abstained. Aside from direct fabrications, the idea that conducting a referendum in the middle of a warzone could elicit honest responses from voters struck many observers as implausible. Reports of Russian soldiers encouraging voters to go to the polls or outright collecting votes on civilians' doorsteps furthered that belief. There were also questions of what territory Russia was actually annexing. Russia did not control the entirety of any of the oblasts. Invading soldiers never captured Zaporizhzhia's capital, and they had just lost control over Kherson's.

Regardless, according to official Russian law, the Kremlin obtained what it needed. On September 30, Putin convened a signing ceremony in Moscow. The Crimean land bridge was now claimed as Russian territory, even if almost no other country recognized it as such.

Ukraine's Ticking Clock

Once again, Ukraine found itself in a time crunch. Mobilizations do not occur overnight. Russia needed time before seeing the benefits of the extra manpower. The question again became whether Ukraine believed that rushing an operation would be better than waiting to find a new opening.

For its part, the Russian mobilization strategy appeared to take on a two-pronged approach. First, some portion of the conscripted men deployed to the frontlines as fast as possible, with only the bare minimum knowledge of how to resist Ukrainian attacks. There were a few points underlying that decision. At a minimum, the frontlines desperately needed more warm bodies. Shifting to a defensive posture facilitated this. The amount of training and knowledge necessary to resist an oncoming attack is less than what it takes to execute an effective offensive operation. Beyond that, Russia's existing troops needed a break. The large frontlines combined with the under-mobilization at the start of the war meant that some Russian soldiers had been fighting without a quiet moment for seven months. Russia pulled back these more experienced troops to regroup for a few weeks, protected them from any further waves of Ukrainian attacks, and put them back to work at a later date.

The second group of Russian troops received a reasonable training regimen. It did not match what Russia's normal conscripts received during peacetime, but they became more than mere cannon fodder. This further put

Ukraine in a race. Now a Russian counterforce would eventually appear. That would partially offset Ukraine's Western-trained brigades set to enter battle in 2023.

On the other side, Ukraine had some structural advantages nudging it toward continuing the counteroffensive, regardless of Russia's mobilization. The troops pushing in Kherson had never stopped, even as the brunt of Ukraine's actions headed north. HIMARS in the region remained constant. Russia never repaired the three bridges leading into Kherson City to the point where resupplies could regularly come in. Russian troops in that section of the oblast remained on a *de facto* island. Worse for them, Moscow's focus had also shifted north, toward stopping the losses east of Kharkiv.

Meanwhile, the city itself had become a theater for partisan warfare. As NBC News' Richard Engel's report *Ukraine's Secret Resistance* details, some of the tactics were age old, while others had a modern flare. The biggest danger for partisans was conducting an attack. However, Ukrainian intelligence had a solution for that problem. The frontlines were close enough that Kherson City sat in artillery range. Waiting soldiers just needed the targets. Thus, Ukraine set up encrypted channels for partisans to discretely pass along the information. One team consisted of a bartender, a taxi driver, and a messenger. The bartender served copious amounts of alcohol to Russian soldiers and listened in as drunken lips disclosed secrets. Meanwhile, the taxi driver had the perfect cover story to travel around the city and spot Russian outposts without raising suspicions. Both passed their information to the messenger, who geolocated the targets on Google Maps and forwarded the coordinates through the encrypted system. Then the artillery blasts rained down.

The counteroffensive campaign had come full circle. What started with an attempt to take Kherson turned into a decisive blow to Russia's efforts to capture Kharkiv. That, in turn, opened up the possibility of converting the Kherson offensive from a failure to a success. But Ukraine still needed a couple of boosts to take it across the finish line.

Nord Stream Sabotage

The first boost came in the middle of Russia's mobilization maneuvers. At 2 am on September 26, European seismologists received reports of what appeared to be a minor tremor. The epicenter was near Bornholm, a Danish island that juts out east into the Baltic Sea, between Sweden and Poland. Seismograph readings were inconsistent with a normal earthquake—it appeared to be an underwater explosion. Contemporaneously, pressure dropped in one of the Nord Stream 2 pipelines. A Danish air team headed to the scene and could observe gas rising to the sea's surface. Something had caused catastrophic damage to the system.

Seven months into the war, Nord Stream had become a deeper political problem. The project was a symbol of Germany's modern-day *Ostpolitik*, literally "eastern policy," referencing West Germany's rapprochement with Eastern Europe during the Cold War. Harkening back to classic theories of economic interdependence, Germany believed that the key to controlling Russian foreign policy was trade. Berlin created a goal of building Russian reliance on German markets. Once achieved, should Moscow pursue unacceptable policies, Berlin would have a new lever to impose stronger economic sanctions. That, in principle, would deter Putin from violating Europe's liberal order.

Problems with this theory came into focus with Russia's invasion of Georgia in 2008. But rather than switch gears, the war became an argument in Berlin for *further* economic integration—Germany did not have enough tools to punish Russia at the time. This paved the way for Nord Stream 1 to open September 2011, creating a direct line for Russian natural gas to flow to Germany. Plans for a second system, the uninspiringly named Nord Stream 2, came to fruition the same year. Berlin wanted Germany to be *the* place for Russian gas exports. The annexation of Crimea merely delayed the system's progress, not shut it down.

Nevertheless, the cracks in *Ostpolitik* were forming. Economic interdependence was a two-way street. Russia relied on German markets for gas, but German businesses relied on Russian gas imports. The costs of conflict had therefore increased for both parties. Russia would be hurt more than before should an economic war begin, but Germany became less inclined to start one given its reliance on Nord Stream. By the end of 2021, the Kremlin was betting that it was in the better relative position. That is, Russia expected that Germany would buckle if Russian troops went further into Ukraine, and the risks were worth the potential reward.

Fast forwarding to 2022, Russia's bet proved wrong. Both Nord Stream projects featured two pipelines running in parallel, with four total lines meant to run Russian gas under the Baltic Sea and to gas-hungry German consumers. Neither of Nord Stream 2's pipelines were running. Construction had finished in the latter half of 2021 and was awaiting final regulatory clearance. The invasion put that on indefinite hiatus. Nevertheless, Germany continued to accept shipments from Nord Stream 1 uninterrupted. This was intended as a stop-gap measure—once Germany had LNG terminals up and running, all Russian imports would end.

Moscow was not pleased. In June 2022, Russia more than halved the flow of Nord Stream 1, alleging that sanctions prevented mechanics from acquiring a Canadian part necessary for the pipeline. The manufacturer of the supposed missing part denied this, leading observers to conclude that Russia was preemptively cutting the flow to increase economic pressure on Berlin. Russia appeared to confirm these suspicions by halving the flow again in July. At the end of August, Nord Stream 1 ceased all deliveries.

That set the scene for September 26. The explosion at 2 am appeared to only affect one of the Nord Stream 2 pipes. Russia had pressurized the pipes to keep the system ready for delivery. Now that gas was rushing through a gaping hole.

Had that been the only event on September 26, it would have drawn international suspicion. Was it an accident or deliberate sabotage? Seventeen hours later, any doubt vanished. Seismographs picked up another series of underwater explosions. This time, Nord Stream 1 was also a victim. The two systems were not connected. This could not be a coincidence. It was sabotage. All told, three of the four pipelines ruptured. Publicly, the earlier pause in gas deliveries within Nord Stream 1 was intended to be temporary, until Germany relented on its coercive pressure toward Russia. The holes in the pipes ensured that Russia would never turn them back on. One of the Nord Stream 2 pipelines remained functional, suggesting that the attack was not a full success. Nevertheless, no one was interested in approving its opening.

The following weeks and months turned the Nord Stream sabotage into one of the world's greatest whodunnit mysteries. Ukrainians had the clearest motive, whether the official government or independent militant factions. Destroying the pipeline guaranteed that Germany and Russia could never reach some type of compromise to turn on the flow and fill Moscow's war coffers. On the other hand, the Baltic Sea was on the other side of Europe. Ukraine had not yet shown the ability to conduct special operations at that distance.

Russia was another leading suspect, despite having built and paid for the pipeline. The logic here was perverse. Perhaps hardliners—be it Putin, the FSB, or someone else—worried that moderates in Russia would push for a withdrawal from Ukraine. A major factor in a hypothetical moderate's calculations was the lost economic productivity by continuing the fight. Destroying the pipe burned the metaphorical bridge. Now even if a moderate attempted to usurp power from Putin, Germany still would not purchase gas from Russia. The location of the attacks raised further suspicion in this regard. The initial explosion occurred within Denmark's exclusive economic zone. The second straddled Denmark's and Sweden's zones. None occurred within their territorial seas. In other words, none of the attacks triggered NATO's Article 5 clause for Denmark. The same would have been true for Sweden, had its NATO application not still been in limbo.

The third group of suspects were collectively the Western countries. Most were against Nord Stream 1's construction, seeing Germany's policy as self-enrichment at the cost of European security. The same criticism followed Nord Stream 2. Three weeks before the war, Biden ramped up the rhetoric during a joint press conference with German Chancellor Olaf Scholz. When asked about the pipelines, Biden said that if Russia invaded, that "there will no longer be a Nord Stream 2." The reporter followed up asking for clarification of what that meant, but Biden offered no further details.

An ambiguous suggestion regarding a hypothetical situation seven months in advance is a long way from an admission of guilt, but it was enough to draw the attention of observers. The motive here was basically the same as Ukraine's. With the pipeline no longer functioning, no one would have to worry that German voters might abandon the coalition. It is even possible that a Western entity did it with the German government's blessing to entrench its position against Russia.

Investigations sprung up by almost all interested parties. However, making clear progress was a challenge—everyone had a conflict of interest, and no one was admitting culpability. Investigators struggled even to narrow down how the sabotage actually occurred. Some level of sophistication was apparent—a significant amount of explosive was necessary to burst the massive pipes, and the multiple hits indicated that the perpetrator was not simply dropping unguided bombs from the surface. Ships routinely passed through that area of the Baltic Sea, and any of them could have sent down dive crews. Indeed, dozens of ships went through with their transponders turned off. But even those were odd suspects—with so many other ships in the area, there was no need to draw extra attention to the guilty ship. It was possible that *none* was responsible and that a more advanced submarine crew had placed the charges.

Months later, at NATO gatherings, the allies adopted a "don't talk about Nord Stream" policy. The consensus was that the outcome was a net positive regardless of who was responsible. Finding evidence that Russia was the guilty party would not have significantly altered public opinion. In contrast, finding evidence that a NATO country was responsible would have been awkward. And discovering Ukrainian culpability would have given dissenting voices within the West ample media fodder. Given that, it was better to let the story die a quiet death.

Whoever was responsible, Ukraine was satisfied with the outcome. If the government sponsored it, then it marked the first major countervalue strike against Russian assets. If the West did it, then some high-level entity was willing to potentially upset its German partners to prove a point about working with Moscow. And if Russia itself laid the explosives, then the Kremlin was in more chaos than anyone knew. It was time to keep up the pressure.

The Crimean Bridge Attack

The world would not wait long for the follow up. At 6 am on October 8, Russians occupying the Crimean

Peninsula received a booming wakeup call: the Crimean Bridge was on fire.

Born out of necessity in 2018, the Crimean Bridge had become a key piece of infrastructure during the war. Russia built it to relieve pressure from Ukraine shutting down the land crossing and damming the North Crimean Canal in 2014. Eight years later, from the outside, the bridge seemed far from superfluous but no longer as critical. Not only was the border open and water flowing through the canal, but Russia had an entire land bridge to reach the peninsula.

Delving deeper into Russian logistics, the Crimean Bridge remained critical to the war effort. The land bridge was of little help to the Russian troops stationed in Kherson on the opposite side of the Dnipro River. The path from Russia through Donetsk and Zaporizhzhia was long. Ukraine had targeted many of those roads as a part of the HIMARS infrastructure campaign, so they were not reliable either. Moreover, rail traffic had a clean path into Kherson from Crimea but not the land bridge. But all that hinged on the Crimean Bridge standing tall.

Beyond those logistical aspects, the Crimean Bridge was an attractive target purely as a countervalue punishment to Moscow. It was a symbol of Russian engineering and Moscow's commitment to the peninsula. When it opened in 2018, Putin drove the first truck across as the headliner of a longer parade. But the bridge's impact was also more tangible. From a financial standpoint, Russia spent a little under $4 billion constructing the bridge, perhaps not a surprising figure given that it was the longest in Europe. Although the Nord Stream sabotage showed that Russian infrastructure was vulnerable, the Crimean Bridge remained the real prize. Ukraine was not shy about this either, with the Ministry of Defense tweeting on August 22 "Kerch Bridge… we are watching you!"

In that light, many wondered why no one had made a play on the bridge before October. Part of this was the high level of difficulty. Even sizable bombs targeting the support structures for the bridge would not have been enough to cause a catastrophic failure. Meanwhile, each section of the roadway was narrow. Hitting it from a distance would be a challenge, and Ukraine lacked an obvious way to get close. Spanning the Kerch Strait, the straightforward solution was to deploy naval assets at it. Once again, the disappearance of Ukraine's navy following Crimea's annexation eliminated that option. The GMLRS rockets for HIMARS could not even get halfway there from the front lines. That left the air force in terms of traditional vectors. Although Ukraine's airmen had done well to beat back the Russian air force at the start of the invasion, such an offensive operation was beyond their capacity. Too much hostile territory stood between the bridge and Ukrainian bases, leaving lots of time for anti-aircraft systems to do their job or for Russia's superior planes to take advantage.

There were also some smaller considerations that disincentivized the bridge's destruction. It acted as a funnel for personnel and equipment coming into the south. The U.S. intelligence community could therefore better monitor what Russian forces had at their disposal, at the cost of more arriving overall. Meanwhile, if Ukraine felt confident in its ability to retake the peninsula, leaving the Crimean Bridge standing had further advantages. Russia had built its own metaphorical golden bridge to retreat from, potentially allowing Ukraine to take the territory without having to fight to the last man. And despite Ukraine's protests about the bridge's construction, the future of an autonomous Ukrainian Crimea relied on compliance among moderates with Russian affinities. The bridge would play a role in that without Ukraine having to finance a new project.

Regardless of those virtues, part of the bridge came tumbling down in the morning hours of October 8. Security tape showed a truck traveling from Russia to Crimea detonate about three-quarters of the way through the trip. The fireball created was enormous. Two sections of the westbound vehicle lanes plunged into the water. The eastbound lanes, part of a separate track on the same support structure, remained standing but had significant charring.

Perhaps most remarkable was the timing. The Crimean Bridge is actually two separate bridges, one for vehicle traffic and one for rail. At the target point, the rail bridge stands many meters higher. The truck detonated just as it converged with a fuel tanker. Despite the distance, the explosion also lit the train on fire, causing significant structural damage to the rail bridge.

Ukraine did not claim responsibility until the following August. But unlike the Nord Stream incident, this time there was an immediate consensus. The explosion was a Ukrainian special forces operation. The details remained vague. But somehow, they acquired substantial quantities of explosives within Russia, managed to pass through security points undetected, and gave Russia one gigantic logistical headache. Official channels celebrated the event even while denying a role. The Ministry of Defense simply tweeted "sick burn" without any context. The Ukrainian postal service, never one to miss a marketing opportunity, released a commemorative stamp. Soldiers giving fingers at Russian ships were out. In were Jack and Rose recreating their iconic Hollywood scene from the bow of the Titanic, with the broken bridge taking the place of the boat.

Although the bridge's support structures remained standing, crossing it became a major pain. On the vehicle side, the westbound lanes needed new spans before any traffic could cross. That left just the two eastbound lanes. Russian operators managed the problem by alternating directional access. For a set period of time, eastbound vehicles could cross. Then new incoming eastbound vehicles had to stop, the traffic had to clear, and afterward westbound vehicles could go. The alternating system meant that flows in both directions could continue but at the cost of great inefficiency. Clearing lanes took time. Traffic began to accumulate at both entrances, as vehicles waited their turn.

Many other factors exacerbated the problem. To begin, the attack demonstrated a then-unknown security vulnerability. Inspections had to ramp up, lest another truck destroy the eastbound lanes. What Russia originally intended to be a normal domestic bridge turned into a crossing similar to an international border. Combined with increased artillery strikes in Crimea, the bridge attack served as a wakeup call to Russophiles on the peninsula. Moscow's hold on the region was no longer guaranteed, and one day it may no longer be possible to drive back to Russia. Outflows therefore increased. At the same time, Ukraine accelerated its pressure on Kherson, placing a greater burden on resupplies heading westward across the bridge. Russia restarted the old ferry system to try to relieve some of the pressure, but the effect was minor.

The rail lines should have compensated for the missing westbound lanes, especially regarding military resupplies. However, Ukraine's fortuitous timing to ignite the oil tanker caused a secondary problem on the rail bridge. Although no spans fell, the heat from the sustained flames left questions about its structural integrity. Russia again found itself down to one functioning pathway. Even then, it restricted access to the line to lighter rail cars. Transporting heavy military convoys featuring tanks and armored personnel vehicles was too risky given the potentially compromised supports.

Retreat from Kherson

Inside the Kremlin, a debate arose on what to do next. From a political standpoint, it appeared that Putin had tied his hands. The September 30 signing ceremony had made Kherson as much a part of Russia as Moscow or Saint Petersburg, at least according to the letter of Russian law. Retreating from the oblast capital would be an embarrassment, just as the earlier retreats up north were. If anything, Russia needed to be going on the offensive and secure the entirety of the oblasts claimed.

At least some portion of Russia's top-level military brass had a more realistic assessment. Ukraine had the initiative. The Kherson offensive never paused even while the more active attacks were ongoing beyond Kharkiv. Ukraine was now rerouting further personnel to the area. The focus thus far aimed inside of the Inhulets River. This was on the Ukrainian side of the *de facto* Kherson island that the Dnipro formed. The Inhulets flowed from the northern most part, closer to the Zaporizhzhia Oblast. Ukraine's strategy appeared to be trying to further isolate Kherson City from the rest of Russia's supply lines.

Eventually, Putin made a change at the top. Russia started the invasion without a senior official in charge of it. Needing better coordination of the evolving battlefield, Putin appointed Aleksandr Dvornikov to the post, likely due to his experience as the first Russian commander of forces in the Syrian Civil War. After the invasion stalled out, Putin sacked him and shifted Gennady Zhidko into the role in May. But Zhidko's inability to hold the north eventually put Sergey Surovikin in charge, a promotion from his position as commander of the southern front.

Surovikin lobbied to retreat from Kherson. The longer Russia waited, the more untenable the situation was becoming. Between the damage to Kherson's bridges, delays at the Crimean Bridge, and partisan sabotage within the city, Russian supply lines could not keep the necessary materiel flowing. Ukraine did not face the same limitations for resupplies to its troops. The resource gap was beginning to show, with Ukraine making slow but progressive advances. By the beginning of November, Ukrainian troops were approaching the town of Snihurivka, a 55-kilometer drive to Kherson.

The risks to Russia were becoming apparent. If Russian troops stayed, encirclement was possible. Scenes from Kharkiv's disorganized retreat, which gifted Ukraine a seemingly endless stream of Russian supplies, would look tame by comparison. For months, Russia had been trying to stockpile as much as it could to defend the city's position. Now it was turning into a potential Ukrainian goldmine. Yet worse for Russia, the decision in September to cover Kherson and leave Kharkiv vulnerable meant that Russia's best troops were concentrating there. If Ukraine could have completed the encirclement, they would have all ended up either captured or killed. Losing Kherson was not supposed to give Ukraine much in the way of a follow-on attack. But if Russia suddenly found itself facing *another* personnel shortage, that could have been a different story.

With that as the backdrop, Surovikin announced that the withdrawal of Russian soldiers to the other side of the Dnipro River would be completed within two days. Ukrainian Defense Minister Oleksii Reznikov expressed skepticism that Russia was physically capable of accomplishing such a logistical feat. Rather, he believed it would take at least a week to pull the estimated 40,000 troops across the river. Yet Surovikin met his goal. Ukrainian troops marched into Kherson on November 11, met by cheering crowds celebrating their liberation.

There was a missed tactical opportunity here for Ukraine. Russian troops had to funnel out of Kherson via the bridges. Ukraine could have responded with an all-out artillery assault on each crossing. That would have trapped the Russian troops, thereby allowing Ukraine to capture or kill tens of thousands. Ultimately, Kyiv chose to let them go—the military advantage was not worth destroying Kherson's infrastructure over the course of a few days of intense urban combat.

On their way out, Russian troops did what their Ukrainian counterparts failed to do back in February: blow the bridge. A span of the Antonivsky Bridge fell into the Dnipro River, dealing a more permanent blow to the passageway than the months of HIMARS strikes had. Ukrainian troops would not be following them any time soon. The countrywide counteroffensive had come to a close.

The Winter Gameplan

Ukraine's successes in Kharkiv and Kherson left the country at a crossroads. Kyiv's troops had exhausted the two obvious angles of attack. A combination of deft maneuvering and superior control of logistics ensured that both ended in great success despite concerns earlier in the summer. But the calendar was turning. The fall rainy season had begun, and next up would be winter. War planners in Kyiv had more decisions to make about how to put the country in the best position it could be for the next phase of the conflict.

In broad strokes, one option was to keep attacking. If Ukraine wanted to pursue this line, a few vectors remained viable. The alternative was to hold back for the winter, attrit Russian forces, and push further advances to the late spring or summer of 2023. Ultimately, the slower option won out. With any luck, the combination of cold temperatures and poor Russian discipline would be more effective at eliminating invaders than a forward-facing assault.

Ukraine's Next Three Targets

One possibility was to maintain the pressure. The upshot here was that Russia was still reeling from its earlier losses. Though Russia had been working on defensive fortifications, Moscow had not yet reached a point of comfort. The fact that the frontlines kept moving both in the north and the south further confounded this process. In addition, Russian mobilization remained ongoing. Continuing to press the issue would have denied some of Russia's advantages in that regard.

To set the stage, over the prior two months, Ukraine had dramatically cut into Russia's territorial possessions. Heading upstream from Kherson, the Dnipro River formed the line of control until the turn in the waterway. At that point, the frontline diverged from the river, running perpendicular west to east. As the line reached Donetsk City, it then shifted north. In effect, the Ukrainian counteroffensives had reduced Russia's gains to the territory adjacent to the eastern Russian border and the Sea of Azov.

Given that positioning, two choices were off the table. Crimea was not an option as a consequence of geography. It hid behind Kherson via land, and the lack of a navy made a sea route irrelevant. More subtly, the core parts of Luhansk and Donetsk were also bad options. They were the areas that the little green men helped turn into separatist regions in 2014. For eight years, Ukraine had already tried reclaiming them as a part of the Donbas War but to no avail. At this point, Russian-aligned forces were too far dug into those positions. Ukraine did not want to let them go, but there was no need to engage in trench battles reminiscent of World War I when better alternatives existed.

Surprisingly, one of those options remained a continuation around Kherson. Yes, the Antonivsky Bridge was no longer passable, and the other crossings were in various states of disrepair. However, Russia still needed to improve its fortifications on the other side of the Dnipro River. In the days following the Russian withdrawal, rumors surfaced of Ukrainian operations along the Kinburn Spit. Spits are thin geographic regions that form as currents pull sand down a line. The Kinburn Spit grew out of the westernmost part of the Crimean land bridge, creating a landing point only a few kilometers away from the rest of Mykolaiv Oblast. This would have given Ukraine a beachhead to attack the remainder of Kherson from a new angle, thereby invalidating many of the entrenchments that Russia was building. Success in the region would have also placed Ukraine on a direct path toward Crimea, which could have been a politically backbreaking loss for the Kremlin.

The second option was Luhansk. This would have avoided the more fortified areas previously under separatist control. Instead, the operation would have been a continuation of September's counteroffensive in the region. Some of Russia's holdings there were fresh from the invasion. Ukraine could have targeted those areas before slowing down the offensive once its soldiers approached the more fortified positions. The upshot here was that that it would have further cut Russian resupplies from the north, allowing Ukraine to use its artillery on resupplies coming from the east.

However, Zaporizhzhia appeared to be the obvious next step. Unlike the other two options, this would have tread new ground. Ukrainian forces had not probed the area since Russia's initial assault. The specific vector would have been just east of the turn in the Dnipro. That would have given Ukrainian forces a land route to drive south. Melitopol, the logistical hub that Russia captured on March 1, was a straight shot in that direction down the E105 highway. The Sea of Azov was slightly further south from there, which would have completely cut the Crimean land bridge in half.

The main strategic advantage of the vector was that success would have opened multiple potential follow-up offensives. A western advance from there was obvious. The damaged metallic Crimean Bridge was temporarily insufficient for resupply, and the attack opened up questions about its further vulnerabilities. Ukraine could have found itself behind the Russian entrenchments facing the Dnipro River as well. Thus, as a first step, Ukraine could have retaken the remainder of Kherson Oblast. From there, its troops could have laid siege to the Crimean Peninsula itself. Geography would then have worked to Ukraine's advantage, as HIMARS would have had a wealth of new targets available once the systems began operating on the opposite side of the Dnipro.

Ukraine also could have headed in the opposite direction, east toward Donetsk Oblast. High value targets were fewer on that side. The focus would have been the port cities of Berdiansk and Mariupol, the latter being the largest city Russia conquered in 2022. That would have put Ukraine back on the *de facto* border with the former Donetsk People's Republic, leading to a natural slowdown as Ukrainian troops tried to break through the trenches.

Nevertheless, the Zaporizhzhia vector came with two major risks. First, if Ukraine did not follow up a drive to the Sea of Azov with further gains, the troops there would have found themselves vulnerable. They would have essentially put themselves in a flanking position for Moscow to exploit, with Russian troops pressuring Ukrainians from both directions of the former land bridge. Russia would have had only a limited amount of time to pull off such a counterattack before its southern supplies dwindled, but the possibility was a concern to Kyiv.

The second problem was the Zaporizhzhia Nuclear Power Plant. It sat an 82-kilometer drive west from the hook in the Dnipro River, slightly closer than the distance to Melitopol. Ukrainian troops would have wanted to push in that direction to follow the river. Doing so would have eliminated one of the directions of potential Russian counterattacks and opened more bridges for faster resupply along the front. It was also a key objective on its own, generating 20% of the country's total electricity before the war. The tradeoff was putting it back into the crosshairs and giving Russia an opportunity to conduct sabotage operations. The same was true further downstream with the Kakhovka Dam and the issues its destruction would have caused on the power plant's cooling systems. Still, Ukraine eventually needed to head toward those targets, so the question was not a matter of the risk so much as when to take that risk.

Of course, all of these potential targets were common knowledge. Russia knew that Ukraine had three good options and that the Zaporizhzhia vector could cause the most problems. And unlike in September, the Kremlin was in a better position to counteract Ukraine's movements. A few months earlier, the Russian army simply was not large enough to protect both Kherson and Kharkiv. Commanders had to pick one and effectively concede the other.

By this point, however, Russia's mobilization was in full swing. The troops heading to the front lines still lacked high-quality training, but they could play effective defense. Ukraine kept close tabs on where they were heading as well as materiel deployments and entrenchments under construction. That level of intelligence gave Ukraine a distinct advantage. Kyiv could see where Russia was most vulnerable. Then, if one vector were suitable compared to holding still for the winter, Ukrainian troops could rush to that location.

Unfortunately for Kyiv, there is an effective counterstrategy under such conditions. The task for Russian planners was to even the odds across each of the possible attack locations. For example, at first pass, it might seem best for Russia to maneuver all available units to Zaporizhzhia. It was the most vulnerable location and thus the most sensible place for Ukraine to attack. However, Ukraine would have seen those units heading in that direction. Recognizing that Russia had more than offset Zaporizhzhia's strategic benefits, Ukrainian troops could have instead headed to the understaffed Kherson or Luhansk lines.

In contrast, if Russia dispersed its troops according to each area's aggregate vulnerability, Ukraine could not take advantage of any one particular mismatch. Indeed, Russia chose a deployment strategy like this. Zaporizhzhia received the bulk of the reinforcements and trench diggers but not all. Some also headed north and south to keep Ukraine honest in those locations. This is why destroying the Antonivsky Bridge did not completely end Kherson as a front. The tougher road ahead there just meant that Russia did not need to place as many troops in the area.

Russia's wise strategy meant that Kyiv's period of maneuver warfare was over. Ukrainian troops could no longer rapidly deploy in vulnerable areas, make substantial gains, and then move to the next location. Ukraine could stay on the offensive and fight through the logistical hurdles that winter was about to bring. But anything further would be a tougher slog.

War of Frozen Attrition

Ukraine's alternative strategy was to hold still. Undoubtedly, choosing this route was a tough pill to swallow. A large portion of the country remained under Russian occupation. If atrocities uncovered as Russia retreated from Kyiv were any indication, Ukrainians living across the line of control were in a world of pain. Then there was the long-term problem of Russia further entrenching its positions and completing its mobilization, soon with well-trained soldiers. The conventional wisdom therefore became that a winter stall would be good for Russia and bad for Ukraine.

Nevertheless, Kyiv ultimately chose the path toward a war of frozen attrition. On the surface, this sounded like the period between the Kyiv offensive and the September Kharkiv counterattack. Back then, Ukraine made little progress, and Russia stabilized after a disastrous start. But winter was not summer. Many observers failed to understand the true nature of the war, leading to public pressure to continue pressing forward. In contrast, Ukraine's war planners set the stage for the weather itself to shift the tide of war. Changes in territorial control would be sparse, but the point was to shape the theater for operations in 2023.

Although the visually interesting parts of any war occur on the battlefield, the decision whether to fight or not is political. In that light, what occurs between any pair of trenches is a series of messages directed to and from the battling countries' capitals. Here, Kyiv wanted to send the signal to Moscow that Russian forces were better off retreating to the original borders. Meanwhile, Moscow was trying to send the signal to Kyiv that Ukrainian forces were better off letting Russia complete the annexation of occupied territories.

That sort of messaging process can take a long time to complete, but it determines the outcome of conflicts more often than not. Few wars end in one side's total military defeat, where that side cannot effectively fight any further. The fall of Nazi Germany during World War II is a rare example. Instead, wars tend to continue until one side decides that prolonging the battle is no longer worthwhile, as compared to what the other side's terms of settlements look like. Outcomes like the United States' departure from the Vietnam War are therefore the more common way to end hostilities. Consequently, winter was not just about winning and losing territory. It was also about shaping Moscow's expectations on what would come later and causing political problems within the Kremlin.

Framing a war of attrition in this light, Russian casualties had an indirect exchange rate with territory. The Kremlin faced challenges in conscripting the hundreds of thousands of soldiers necessary to stabilize the border. Casualties, even with no immediate change in territorial control, could have caused further domestic strife. Even if that were not enough to force a withdrawal, it might have given the Kremlin second thoughts about instituting another round of mobilization. Eventually, Ukraine's hope was that Russia would hit another personnel shortage, at which point the accumulation of casualties would have turned into territorial gains for Ukraine.

The key was to turn winter into an ally to facilitate a favorable casualty ratio over that period. Thoughts of winter and war often conjure up images of literal and figurative frozen conflicts, with both sides taking a timeout before resuming hostilities once the temperatures rise. Although it is true that cold weather slows direct military confrontations, this interpretation misunderstands the earlier point about how wars are battles of political will. Each side exerts costly effort to eliminate the other side, which alters a leader's calculus on whether to continue.

Think about how winter affects these actions. Movement remains possible. It is just more difficult to trudge through snow. The speed of infantry might be cut in half, for example. If the ground does not completely freeze—as was the case during the February 2022 invasion—then vehicles must move slowly to guarantee they do not get stuck in the *rasputitsa*. In wooded operation zones, trees become barren, helping defenders to aim their crosshairs at oncoming attacks. In sum, militaries can still conduct offensive operations. They just need to exercise greater caution.

Consequently, Russia and Ukraine could not leave the frontlines unguarded. As tempting as it was to retreat to the warmth of a cabin and fireplace, some portion of troops had to stay vigilant out in the elements. Otherwise, the other side could have ignored the weather, strolled on in, and made good progress despite the apparent hurdles. Thus, the two sides remained lined up in the cold. They still worried about opposing fire. But if they were not careful, they could also succumb to the temperature. Everyone was all the more miserable as a result.

At the end of the day, though, each side was still exerting costly effort. Each side still wanted to eliminate the other side. Each side persisted in manipulating the opposing leader's resolve to stay in the battle. In other words, war continued. It was just war by other means. The key difference was that cold weather would pick its winners and losers through a new process. Ukraine's maneuver warfare was not the same powerful tool it was just a couple of months earlier. Now the difference between success and failure turned to rotation and logistics.

Rotations counteract winter cyclically. Even when the weather is pristine, soldiers still need to rotate off the frontlines periodically. Failure to do so leads to combat fatigue and perhaps literal fatigue from sleep deprivation. Winter intensifies those problems. Psychologically, the cold saps morale. Physically, it causes frostbite. Fading back from the frontlines, even for hours at a time, warms up the soldiers and helps keep them in fighting shape.

Russia had already experienced problems with rotation before winter set in. The original 200,000 troops in Ukraine were insufficient to allow for regular rotations. The Russian frontlines suffered as a consequence, which Ukraine exploited during its counteroffensive. These problems continued for Russia during the early phases of winter. However, as forces from the September mobilization streamed in, Russia found itself in a better position—so much so that Moscow had designs on a new offensive.

The attempt occurred around the town of Vuhledar and was short-lived. With a pre-war population of only 14,000, the location itself did not matter much. Rather, it represented an attempt to push beyond the 2014 lines to the southwest of Donetsk City. Further, its high ground would have helped give artillery control over the T-0509 highway. Toward the end of January 2023, Russian troops began accumulating outside of it and engaging in localized combat. But the main event began in early February, when dozens of tanks and armored vehicles approached. The engagement ended in a bloodbath. It seemed as if the tank units had forgotten the lessons from the Kyiv offensive, when columns of metal became easy pickings for Ukrainian defenders.

Almost everywhere else—with a key exception that the next chapter focuses on—the fighting occurred on a lower level. Along the front, Ukraine retained two structural advantages that it tried to exploit throughout the winter. First, Ukraine was playing on its home field. It was possible for Ukrainian soldiers to not only depart from the frontlines but also briefly take leave to see their friends and family, which helped keep morale high. The distances involved for Russian troops to do the same were prohibitive. Furthermore, there was a political problem. Russian troops could communicate to their loved ones that the reality of the "special military operation" was not as it seemed. Some might even try to desert when called on to return. Meanwhile, more local rotations also favored Ukraine. Ukrainians lived on either side of the frontlines. Thus, when Ukrainian troops went back to the nearest small town or village, they could relax and enjoy some hospitality. In contrast, Russian soldiers had to stay on guard and worry about partisan attacks.

Second, the vast majority of fighting in the war up to that point had occurred east of the line of control. Damage to infrastructure was therefore greater in the locations Russia had available for shelter than Ukraine had. The advantage was not as pronounced in the areas near the Kharkiv counteroffensive. But even then, Ukraine's rapid gains minimized damage to housing.

The second structural advantage winter brought was in logistics. Surviving winter requires an influx of supplies. This begins with clothing. Anyone who has lived in cold weather climates knows just how much of a difference a layer or two of thermals makes. Although Eastern Ukraine is far from the Siberian Arctic, days could pass before the temperature ever went above freezing. Surviving such a climate requires heavier jackets at a minimum. No matter what the mercury reads, high-tech equipment is great. But an opposing army with antiquated weapons can simply wait out the winter if it is the only one with sets of fleece undergarments and overcoats. September's mobilization highlighted Russia's problems in this regard. Conscripted soldiers received orders to bring their own equipment, as Moscow struggled to issue even basic uniforms. Winter would test those problems further.

However, clothing was just the start. Heaters are necessary to generate warmth and combat cases of frostbite or hypothermia when they develop. Those require batteries to run. Unfortunately, batteries are less effective in colder temperatures, so winter armies need even more batteries. Cold temperatures force humans to burn more calories to stay warm. In turn, soldiers' minimum daily caloric needs rise, meaning more food—and hopefully hot food—has to arrive on the frontlines. Transporting all of this requires fuel. And then they need more fuel for the rotations and to run the vehicle's heating systems. Whether by design or not, the damage to the Crimean Bridge—central for resupply along the southern tier—could not have come at a worse time for Russia.

Russia's Discipline Problem

As winter continued, Ukraine took advantage of one final asymmetry between the two countries: military discipline. Obtaining victory in war requires a team effort—no lone Russian was about to capture Kyiv or any regional capital by himself. However, the incentives for individual soldiers do not always align with the group. Ukraine aimed to exploit the asymmetry throughout the winter.

More generally, political scientists call this type of situation a "collective action problem." Each individual has to choose whether to exert effort, take an action, or *not* engage in some sort of self-centered behavior. Doing so forces the individual to make a sacrifice or incur a risk each would otherwise not have to bear. Fortunately, the benefits to the group for undertaking such pro-social behaviors are enormous. However, the individual only internalizes a small portion of those benefits. If individuals only care about themselves, then they calculate that the costs of the pro-social behavior outweigh their personal rewards. Consequently, none of them engages in it. The result is that everyone is worse off than had each individual made a personal sacrifice.

Littering is a classic example of the principle. Holding onto your trash until you find the proper receptacle incurs a small cost on you. The benefit you internalize by doing so is small because it is unlikely you will ever encounter a particular piece of trash again. However, the cumulative effect of everyone else seeing the mess that you caused is large. If everyone is selfish, then litter goes everywhere and creates a giant eyesore. The group may collectively agree that everyone would individually be better off if each person used trash cans as they should. Unfortunately, among selfish individuals, no one person has an incentive to follow through on that. Even if everyone else were going to use the trash cans, the individual prefers to litter rather than suffer the inconvenience of waiting to find one.

The battlefield is rife with collective action problems, especially during winter. As temperatures plunge, soldiers exposed to the elements on the frontlines might get desperate to stay warm. A simple solution is to light a fire. The problem there is that doing so effectively sends a signal flare to opposing artillery. Now the entire unit is dead. Here, lighting the fire is an anti-social behavior. It benefits the individual directly in front of it but imposes great risks to everyone else around due to incoming enemy fire. Even though the person lighting the fire is also subject to that risk, he may personally prefer being warm.

Another "solution" to the cold is to drink alcohol. Vodka consumption among Russian soldiers stationed along the border prior to the invasion was already a problem; the weather and stress from combat only exacerbated it. However, the relief only goes to the person drinking. Every other soldier in the unit becomes more vulnerable because the inebriated individual loses the ability to defend against an oncoming attack. Worse yet, the personal benefit for drunkenness is fleeting. The reason that alcohol makes a person feel warmer is because it opens up blood vessels, allowing more blood to reach the skin. But Mother Nature immediately saps that warmth, causing the person's core temperature to drop. In extreme conditions—like what was present on the battlefield—this can be lethal.

Of course, the easiest way to stay warm is to never get cold. But this creates a perverse incentive and further discipline problems. Imagine that a commander tells a soldier to go out on a scouting mission or do a perimeter patrol. The soldier then has two options. Option one is to follow orders, get cold, and risk death. That last possibility was a bigger concern in this war than in previous due to the advent of the digital battlefield. In the past, artillery might not bother targeting a lone scouter even if spotted—the odds of hitting him were low and therefore might not have justified the cost of the shell. Now drones provide precise, real-time coordinates, which makes artillery substantially more accurate. Some drones—so-called "loitering munitions"—skipped the middle step by arming a basic quadcopter with small grenades. Once their controllers spot the lone scouter, they simply fly over the target, release the payload, and go for the kill.

Option two is to feign compliance, stay in, stay warm, and survive. Absent any other concerns, this was the obvious best choice for a soldier. However, such inaction compounded the problem for Russian command. Feigned patrols were worse than doing nothing. Noncomplying soldiers could convince commanders that the coast was clear, leading to suboptimal battlefield strategies down the line.

Governments are well aware of the issues that collective action problems raise in militaries. Unfortunately for the Kremlin, resolving them was difficult. The most elegant solution is to shift the ideology of soldiers. This is essentially cultural persuasion. If the government can convince its citizens of the utility of the goal at hand, soldiers might reduce how they internalize self-sacrifice. That is, they begin to view the costs and risks of death to themselves as acceptable because the broader group effort is worthwhile. From a compliance standpoint, this is the easiest solution. It does not require any further monitoring mechanisms. Soldiers just do what commanders want them to do because the soldiers *want* to do it.

The Kremlin engaged in a long effort with ideological persuasion in the lead up to Ukraine. Putin's July 2021 essay entitled "On the Historical Unity of Russians and Ukrainians" epitomized this strategy. In it, he argued that Russians, Ukrainians, and Belarusians are actually a single people that should be under one government. Upon publication, the Kremlin built a brief media blitz around the essay. Although it may have influenced some Russian minds, it did not have the impact that the Kremlin had hoped.

Indeed, the ideological front created a significant asymmetry in the war. Average Ukrainians on the front lines knew what they were fighting for. For the average Russian, the same question was ambiguous. Ukraine took advantage of this by setting up a surrender hotline. Russians could call it to obtain information on how to exit the frontlines and enter a Ukrainian prisoner of war camp without risking injury or death.

Another classic solution is automaticity. Here, the military attempts to train soldiers to not think about incentives at all, be it their own or the state's overall goals. Rather, they need to become cogs in a greater machine—cogs that only work to fulfill their commanded purpose. This is in part why drill instructors grill new recruits for an untold number of hours each day. Any deviation from orders receives a stiff response. Eventually, instructors hope to break down the psychological barrier so that any calculations out of self-interest or otherwise simply stop happening.

Reaching that point is difficult for any military—humans did not evolve to easily forget about their own mortality. Russia appeared to fail in this process well before the war, with corruption and graft as hallmarks of its military system. It did not get better after the September 2022 mobilization. The portion of troops that immediately deployed to the frontlines never had the opportunity to go through that process. Those that received training still plowed through it, not at the pace necessary to instill any kind of automaticity.

Absent solutions at the personal level, militaries can still overcome collective action problems with strict monitoring and enforcement. There may be incentives to skip a patrol to stay warm and stay alive, but commanding officers can counteract that. Reports of Russian troops being withheld food or suffering beatings at the hands of other Russians were commonplace. This changes a shirking soldier's calculus. Yes, faking a patrol may be in that person's short-term self-interest. However, looking at the situation more holistically, a small risk of death and temporarily losing feeling in one's fingertips is preferable to not eating for a week or having one's ribs broken.

Of course, the enforcement part also requires effective monitoring. Ukraine took action to make that complicated for Russia. Earlier on during the war, the Kremlin attempted to resolve discipline problems by stationing high-level commanders close to the frontlines. In theory, they could oversee dereliction of duty and mismanagement. Moreover, unlike their lower-level comrades, their positions were well-compensated—or at least put them in positions to accept substantial bribes. Either way, they had good reason to keep the enlisted and early career officers in line.

Still, that required the generals to stay alive. Within the first three months of the war, Ukraine had three confirmed kills of generals: Andrei Sukhovetsky allegedly near Hostomel, Vladimir Frolov under uncertain circumstances, and Kanamat Botashev in Luhansk. Ukraine also claimed Andrei Simonov as a fourth, though with no confirmation. Losing just one general is a big deal. Losing two, especially over such a short period, is rare. Losing three is exceptional. By comparison, the United States lost only five in combat during the entirety of the Vietnam War. Ukraine also claimed six other kills, though those would receive varying levels of skepticism. Regardless, the Kremlin recognized that the cure was worse than the disease and began pulling back their generals to safer locations.

The other key problem Ukraine caused was decentralization. HIMARS attacks continued through the summer and into the winter, again aiming to inhibit Russian logistics. In response, Russia decentralized some of its supply depots to limit the damage that any single attack could inflict. But this further restricted the high-level staff's ability to monitor low-level troops' good behavior. Depots contained supplies worth millions of dollars on the black market. They could not go unprotected. However, policing corruption is much easier when everything is centralized at a single site. In contrast, decentralization forced anti-corruption patrols to bounce around from site to site, opening opportunities for bad behavior when they were not around.

The culmination of all of these problems was the Makiivka military quarters shelling, occurring as the clocks were about to strike midnight on December 31. Makiivka was connected to Donetsk City through urban sprawl, part of what the separatists captured in 2014. Russian troops had assembled at Professional Technical School No. 19 to celebrate the new year. The gathering violated a number of safety measures. Too many Russian soldiers were in the same place, making it a tempting artillery target for Ukraine. Moreover, the celebration occurred on top of an ammunition dump.

However, worst of all was phone discipline. Some soldiers had access to their mobile phones and made unauthorized calls home to wish their loved ones a happy new year. It had all the trappings of a collective action problem. Talking to one's own family only benefited that individual. But it imposed risks on the entire group, as an intercepted call could give away their position to Ukrainian artillery. And indeed, the Russian Defense Ministry believed this was exactly what happened.

At 11:57 pm, the first HIMARS rocket came in. Three more subsequently arrived, the last just one minute into 2023. The casualties were significant. Russia admitted that there were 89 deaths. Ukraine's initial estimate was 400, though an intercepted phone call later put that number at 610. Regardless, the situation was a disaster.

Nevertheless, it was not the main event of the winter…

The Battle of Bakhmut and the Wagner Opera

The city of Bakhmut became the centerpiece of the winter campaign, if for no other reason than it was the only place where the lines on maps were changing. It was an unassuming municipality about 96 kilometers east of Luhansk and 70 kilometers north of Donetsk, just past some of the original separatist areas. The battle itself began on August 1, 2022. Over the next few weeks, Russia made steady gains. However, by early September, Ukraine's Kharkiv counteroffensive dominated the headlines. Then the Kherson counteroffensive continued to draw attention away from Bakhmut.

By the time Bakhmut made it into the spotlight, the battle had already devolved into costly trench warfare. In the end, that trench warfare turned into urban warfare and had all the trappings of a meatgrinder. But no one anticipated that it would spiral into the biggest challenge to Putin's authority in his 23-year tenure, never mind how it would end.

Why Bakhmut?

Part of the public's fascination with Bakhmut stemmed from bewilderment. Why did a city of seemingly so little importance become the site of the potentially deadliest battle of the entire war? The question's premise was accurate. Despite a two-month battle for it in 2014 and a much longer one between 2022 and 2023, Bakhmut had little direct strategic value. Its pre-war population was only 71,000, and that number dwindled into the hundreds as the battle destroyed just about every building in the city. Strategically, it was low ground, subject to artillery fire from surrounding areas. And although a number of highways intersected with Bakhmut, it was not the logistics hub that Melitopol or other cities were.

As time passed, commentators increasingly explained that the Battle of Bakhmut was important *because it was important.* The absence of other developments in the war made it the media's centerpiece for months on end. For either side to concede the city to the other would be a major political black eye. Thus, even in the face of rising casualties, both sides pressed on.

The problem with that thinking is that it does not explain why the battle started in the first place. Answering that question then reveals a more satisfying reason for why it continued: the Kremlin appeared to lack any better option. The war had dug Putin into a hole. What was supposed to be a rapid special military operation became anything but, requiring a large mobilization to steady Russian holdings on Ukraine's eastern flank. The official annexation ceremony further meant that Russia did not control areas that Russian law dictated were under Moscow's authority. Failing to reach at least that far might not guarantee an end to Putin's regime, but it would rally challengers. Perhaps signaling that need to go on the offensive, Putin demoted Sergey Surovikin, the architect of the Kherson withdrawal, in January 2023. Valery Gerasimov, Russia's Chief of the General Staff for all armed forces, took on a second role as the commander of the invasion.

However, going on the offensive was no simple task. Ukraine still held portions of Luhansk, Donetsk, Zaporizhzhia, and Kherson Oblasts. Luhansk was a nonstarter after Russia lost ground in the September counteroffensive. Kherson was even worse now that the November counteroffensive put Russia behind the Dnipro River. That left just Zaporizhzhia and Donetsk. Russia tried assaults in both places. It just so happened that Donetsk—

and specifically Bakhmut—was the only place where Russian troops could move forward.

As for the mounting casualties, Putin seemed to be engaging in an archetypical wartime behavior known as "gambling for resurrection." If a leader fears that the war outcomes thus far have made his grip of power tenuous, he may take risks that a fresh leader would never even consider. Losing may make the situation worse but not much worse than it already is—at least in terms of the leader's political fortunes. In contrast, if the gamble pays off, he successfully resurrects his career.

By analogy, it would be weird to see someone walk into a casino and place his entire life savings on black at the roulette table. It would start to make sense if that person explained how he owed the mob tens of thousands of dollars, and the only way to obtain that money before it comes due is through the roulette wheel. If it lands on red, he is dead—but he is also dead through inaction, so that does not matter much. On the other hand, if it lands on black, he is safe.

Here, the mob was Russian political challengers, whether within the Kremlin or revolutionary masses. The roulette wheel was Bakhmut. And black and red were the results coming from the battlefield.

The Wagner Opera's Opening Act

Another reason the Battle of Bakhmut became so fascinating was how Russia pursued the action. Its traditional military was there, but the focal actor was the Wagner Group. Founded in 2014, it encapsulated the bizarre duality of Russian military politics. By law, private military companies (or PMCs) were illegal in Russia. Yet the Wagner Group persisted. Moreover, as far as Western analysts could tell, the Kremlin appeared to be financing the operation.

For eight years, the Wagner Group stayed out of the spotlight. Those following Russia's geopolitical adventures, however, were well-aware of its importance. The Wagner Group functioned as a *de facto* expeditionary force. Experienced Russian soldiers who would have otherwise cycled out of the official armed forces instead signed lucrative contracts with the PMC. Initially, the group grew out of the "little green men" who fomented rebellion in the Donbas. As the active portion of that conflict drew to a close, Wagner forces found themselves defending Russian interests in the Syrian Civil War. A couple of years later, they deployed to Africa, providing security for governments struggling to stay in power. Their successes not only stabilized Russian-friendly regimes, they also came with a hefty share of the natural resource rights that funded those governments.

Such a PMC came with many benefits for the Kremlin as well. First, at least before the Battle of Bakhmut, using the Wagner Group created a smokescreen of plausible deniability. If something went wrong, or a mission required breaking various international laws, the Kremlin could stay out of the picture. Kremlin press officers could explain that, yes, Russian citizens were responsible for those activities. But they were not the Kremlin's official forces. They were a private company engaging in geopolitical affairs independent of the Russian government. Any issues with their activities should be brought to the attention of Wagner leadership and not to the Kremlin. The same plausible deniability was also helpful within Russia. If an operation failed and many mercenaries died, no one could blame the Kremlin. Again, the government never ordered them to do anything. They were just private contractors who made some mistakes leading to their deaths.

Second, the broader creation of PMCs within Russia represented acceptance of the Ministry of Defense's own failures to craft an effective fighting force. High levels of corruption doomed the plans for a three-day assault on

Kyiv. Fully fixing those problems required bureaucratic reforms at a level that would be difficult for any country. Worse for the Kremlin, the measures discussed in previous chapters failed to meet the mark. PMCs represented a way to start anew. They also created strong incentives for leadership to work hard. Putin could essentially structure the system as an internal competition. The better their performance, the more resources the Kremlin could pass along. Those that failed could meet a swift end—after all, PMCs were illegal.

Third, dividing military power within a country is a common coup-proofing tactic. Whenever an autocrat creates a military force, he begins a guardianship dilemma as well. More powerful militaries better coerce the country's foreign rivals. However, the military can also turn much of that strength against the leader. Thus, autocrats must get creative to find ways to give the country an international presence while not facilitating a military coup.

A simple solution to this problem is to section off military power. If no single group can dominate the others, then initiating a coup becomes more difficult. The leading entity must coordinate with the others to ensure that enough are onboard to guarantee the coup's success. That can be a challenge given that loyalists can inform the leader about whispers of a coup plot, which then gives the leader time to adopt countermeasures.

For Russia, this solution ran deep. There were the traditional armed forces, which decentralized some of its recruitment practices and supply procurement to the individual oblasts. The 141st Special Mobilized Regiment, actually the private army of Chechen governor Ramzan Kadyrov, is the best example of this. Then there is the most famous of the PMCs, the Wagner Group. But other PMCs existed as well, including a prominent one named Patriot, which had ties to Defense Minister Sergei Shoigu. Even

Gazprom, Russia's main energy company, employed its own PMC.

Wagner in Bakhmut

Despite years of experience, what Wagner planned to do in Bakhmut was unprecedented in Russian PMC history. In the past, Wagner mostly acted like special forces, conducting limited attacks and advising client states. In Bakhmut, they were to function as an extension of the Russian army. That meant manning trenches, conducting waves of attacks, and generally trying to gain territory one meter at a time.

This was a bloody process. Without taking extraordinary measures, it would have gutted the Wagner Group's core. That was a major concern for both Wagner leadership and Moscow. The Russian armed forces more generally struggled to maintain a cadre of noncommissioned officers. Again, part of the point of Wagner was to maintain military knowledge. When bureaucratic forces would cycle those soldiers out of the military, the Wagner Group would step in. Consequently, the average Wagner mercenary was highly skilled. To use them as cannon fodder would be a waste of a scarce resource.

In September 2022, the world witnessed Wagner's solution to the problem, in video form straight from the lips of the soon-to-be-infamous Yevgeny Prigozhin. Before that point, Prigozhin was publicly known as "Putin's chef," having gained prominence within the Kremlin by providing catering contracts. However, Western intelligence long suspected that Prigozhin was much more than that—a personal operative for Putin, overseer of the Internet Research Agency's social media influence and disinformation campaigns, and a founder of the Wagner Group. After eight years of Prigozhin's denials, the video provided confirmation of that last role, and he acknowledged his position in Wagner later in the month.

His origin story aside, the video featured Prigozhin in a Russian prison yard offering the convicted criminals there a deal. Anyone who served six months with Wagner would receive a pardon and go free—assuming they survived the frontlines. This was still the middle of Russia's manpower shortage that the September 22 mobilization announcement would partially alleviate, but the program continued well beyond that point. The Battle of Bakhmut required relentless assaults on Ukrainian positions, and Wagner wanted the prisoners to serve as the cannon fodder.

Of course, prisoners were not the most dependable of mercenaries. Their incentives were a battle between time and death—as long as they could survive for six months while appearing to do their duty, the rules stated that they could go home free. By comparison, all of the earlier compliance problems Russia had to deal with looked easy. Now Wagner was in charge of a bunch of convicts turned quasi-soldiers—not exactly the group of people with pro-social attitudes an officer would want under his command.

Consequently, Wagner had to adapt its battlefield plans to the constraints at hand. What resulted were probing runs that defined the Battle of Bakhmut. At any point in time, Russia had a few plausible vectors of attack to choose from. Perhaps a gas station, a winery, or a garbage dump—all actual places in Bakhmut that Ukraine and Russia spent ample time fighting over. Russia would begin a probing run by peppering those areas with artillery to soften the targets. The first wave of soldiers—often the convicts—had clear orders. They were to attack the areas until they captured the land or became physically unable to do so, whether by serious injury or death. Under no circumstances could they try returning early. If anyone did, anti-retreat Russian forces would execute them on the spot. Nor were they permitted to surrender.

Wagner meant business with the standing no-surrender order. Yevgeny Nuzhin was a 55-year-old convict-soldier deployed to Luhansk in late August 2022. His military career did not last long, as he surrendered to Ukrainian forces on September 4. While in custody, he gave multiple interviews criticizing the Russian war effort. By November, however, he was back in Wagner's hands. How that happened is unclear—it is possible he was part of a prisoner exchange, though the official Wagner account contends that the group kidnapped him while he was still in Ukraine. Regardless, on November 13, a video surfaced of Nuzhin's execution via sledgehammer to the head. It was a warning to others: if you surrender to Ukrainians, you will ultimately receive an even worse fate.

Even with fully committed soldiers attacking to the death, most of the vectors they pursued would likely fail. This was still not a total loss for Russia—Ukraine would have to reveal the location of its artillery in the meantime, allowing Russia to hit those targets with counter-artillery fire. If there was a success, say at the winery, Russia held a second wave of attackers in reserve. Unlike the cannon fodder, these were more experienced soldiers. They would deploy to the winery, hoping that Ukraine would be caught flat-footed there.

Using these human wave attacks, Russia made incremental gains but at a brutal cost. On January 6, 2023, the town of Soledar fell to Russian forces. Named for the salt mine that dominated its economy, it was the final major stop heading northeast to southwest toward Bakhmut proper. Eighteen kilometers later, Russia would be battling in Bakhmut's streets.

Wagner versus the Kremlin

Back in Kyiv, Zelensky kept a close eye on developments in Bakhmut. Ukraine was also taking heavy losses. U.S. intelligence believed that the city was a lost cause and encouraged Kyiv to order a retreat. Once Russia entered the city, Ukrainian troops could use the high ground they still held to rain down artillery. Zelensky declined the advice, choosing instead a much slower withdrawal. For weeks on end, observers declared that "Bakhmut holds" even as it became apparent that its fall was only a matter of time.

The calculus in Kyiv was one of raw numbers. There was no doubt that Ukrainian troops were taking heavy losses. But the question remained whether Russian losses were worse. To justify the stand in Bakhmut, the ratio needed to be very favorable. A simple one-to-one trade put Ukraine on the losing end, given that an experienced Ukrainian soldier had greater military value than a former prisoner with a rifle. But if so, it played right into the hands of Kyiv's winter plan. It was still a waiting game for the Western-trained battalions to return. Ukraine did not mind losing fragments of territory to stall for time, especially if the opposing losses left Russia vulnerable to a later counteroffensive. The fact that Russia had a larger population and more troops theoretically in reserve did not concern Kyiv. Putin's September 2022 mobilization announcement left the Kremlin in an uneasy political position, and it was unclear whether Russia could bring more forces into Ukraine.

Whether Ukraine succeeded in that goal to create a favorable casualty ratio was the subject of a debate. Each side treated the casualty ratio as a state secret, with both predictably claiming that the other had it worse. Anonymous NATO officials indicated it was five-to-one in Ukraine's favor. Leaked documents from the Pentagon seemed to confirm that number in April; humorously, pro-Russian influencers digitally swapped the numbers in the leaked photos to make the ratio appear flipped in Russia's favor. The ratio was dropping as winter turned to spring, though. This was a problem because even a seemingly good ratio belied the aforementioned quality tradeoff. As such, the declining ratio signaled that Ukraine needed to rethink its strategy.

Another sign that the overall Bakhmut strategy favored Ukraine came from an unexpected source: Wagner's leader Yevgeny Prigozhin. Since the Kharkiv counteroffensive, Prigozhin had become increasingly critical of the Russian Ministry of Defense's prosecution of the war. He was a rare voice among the disaffected, as criticism of the special military operation was a criminal offense. Even referring to it as a "war" risked jailtime. But somehow, Prigozhin avoided punishment—at least for the moment.

As winter wore on, Prigozhin's messages escalated to an open war of words against Shoigu and Gerasimov. As the minister of defense and chief of staff respectively, they were at the center of the Ministry of Defense's war planning. That did not stop Prigozhin from repeatedly using slurs in reference to them. The central issue was artillery shells. From Prigozhin's perspective, the Kremlin was starving Wagner of the shells it needed to achieve final victory in Bakhmut, despite his forces being the only ones making real progress over the winter.

Behind the scenes, the public spat had all the markings of an internal power struggle. Both Prigozhin and the Ministry of Defense wanted to curry favor with Putin, who had been uncharacteristically quiet on the subject. If Shoigu and Gerasimov viewed Prigozhin as a political threat, then they had an active incentive to undermine Wagner's success in Bakhmut. And the battle appeared to be culminating. On April 3, Russian forces claimed they captured Bakhmut's town hall. Three days later, it was the rest of the city center.

Suddenly, though, it seemed that Russia was about to snatch defeat from the jaws of victory. By the end of April, Prigozhin declared that he was ready to withdraw Wagner troops from Bakhmut, with Ukraine still engaging Russian forces at the city's edge. On May 5, he made a clear ultimatum. Using rows of deceased and visually mutilated Wagner personnel as a background, Prigozhin blamed the Ministry of Defense for what he saw as unnecessary deaths.

The threat was simple: if Wagner did not receive sufficient ammunition and artillery, the group would leave. Some type of intervention convinced him to stay to finish the job. On May 20, Prigozhin declared the city Russia's and began an organized process to transfer its control to regular Russian forces. Thirteen days later, he announced Wagner's controlled withdrawal.

Ukraine had not yet given up on Bakhmut, with successful counterattacks along the city's northern and southern flanks. Nevertheless, the Wagner mercenaries were no longer going to participate in day-to-day combat. Instead, they withdrew east, staying within Donetsk to watch the battle at arm's length.

Wagner's Thunder Run

The internal rivalry was not over from the Ministry of Defense's perspective, though. Prigozhin claimed that Russian regulars had mined Wagner's withdrawal route, intentionally trying to kill the group's personnel. The Ministry of Defense denied the accusation but clarified its underlying goals with a mid-June declaration. All of Russia's bizarrely fragmented military organizations—Wagner included—had to return to centralized command. Fighters could continue battling in the war, but their contracts had to come straight from the Ministry of Defense.

For Prigozhin, this was a red line. It was not just about losing his leadership role within the context of the invasion. Wagner also had a large number of *de facto* business dealings in Africa. If the Ministry of Defense were to exert control over *all* militant organizations as suggested, Wagner would no longer have a functional business model. That did not sit well with Prigozhin. And after a wild sixteen months of war, he felt compelled to initiate the craziest 24 hours of it that anyone had seen.

The tale began on the afternoon of June 23, 2023. Prigozhin first released a video lecture that gave Russians a sobering look at the war—the high casualty counts, the poor planning, and the general lack of success. As usual, the Ministry of Defense was the target. Many of his previous statements went far beyond what Russian authorities normally tolerated, but this one reached a new level of criticism. Come the evening, the real action began. Prigozhin distributed a second video, this one of the apparent aftermath of Ministry of Defense missile strikes on Wagner. He claimed that it was a deliberate act to destroy his forces—though analysts were unsure whether any of the alleged attack was authentic.

Regardless of the truth, Prigozhin used it as a *casus belli.* Wagner troops departed from Donetsk and travelled east to Rostov-on-Don, a city inside Russia that served as the main Russian base of operations for the Eastern front. The city immediately fell, with virtually no resistance from regular Russian forces or Rostov-on-Don's traditional police. As Wagner planted landmines to protect against the Kremlin's response, civilians took to the streets to welcome their apparent new leadership. If anyone wanted the group gone, they were unwilling to make it known.

Active rebellion against the Russian state at this level had never occurred during the Putin era. Protests occurred intermittently and had the ability to change policy, with the aftermath of Putin's 2018 attempt to reform the pension program a notable example. But this was different. A rebellious paramilitary had captured an entire city. Prigozhin released recordings of him continuing his discussion of grievances with a deputy defense minister and deputy chief of staff from the local command headquarters. Western observers began wondering whether the war in Ukraine might see a sudden end. Some Ukrainian soldiers literally began popping popcorn as they watched the news, even as Prigozhin announced that he was not going to interfere with Rostov-on-Don's resupply missions. The mixed messaging left observers wondering what Prigozhin had planned for his endgame.

In the morning hours of June 24, Wagner raised the stakes. A convoy of trucks, armored vehicles, and tanks began driving toward Moscow, seemingly to stage a coup against Putin's regime. Many of Wagner's forces stayed behind in Rostov-on-Don—including Prigozhin—but thousands participated in the thunder run. And its pace was brisk. By midday, the convoy had reached Voronezh, halfway to the Kremlin. Russian regular forces offered little resistance. Some may have even joined. The Russian Air Force fired on the convoy from the skies, but Wagner came prepared with anti-aircraft weaponry. The convoy continued undeterred, shooting down a helicopter and a command-center plane as it went.

Meanwhile, the Kremlin was uncharacteristically silent. Putin did not release a statement following the capture of Rostov-on-Don and waited until 10 am the next day before addressing the convoy, calling on Wagner troops to stand down. Municipal authorities in Moscow began making preparations to defend the city. Speculation that Russia would devolve into a civil war further mounted.

And then… it just ended. The convoy turned around and returned to Rostov-on-Don. Belarus announced that it had brokered a deal between Prigozhin and the Kremlin. Officially, Russia granted all Wagner participants amnesty, including Prigozhin. The Ministry of Defense's centralization program would continue. Wagner mercenaries had to decide between signing a contract or fleeing to the group's new base in Belarus. By 11 pm, Prigozhin began pulling out of Rostov-on-Don. But it remained clear where latent support in the region was—a crowd formed around Prigozhin's vehicle, with the onlookers wishing him well wherever he ultimately ended up.

Western intelligence reports in the aftermath of the thunder run provided some insight into what actually happened. Prigozhin wanted to attempt a mutiny against Russian military leadership but not a coup against Putin's civilian government. He had indications that Minister of Defense Sergei Shoigu and Chief of Staff Valery Gerasimov would be in Rostov-on-Don. This was not far from Wagner's post-Bakhmut operating base in Donetsk. Wagner could blitz there and arrest them. Details are fuzzy about what Prigozhin would do next. But once the pair were captured, the status quo would shift in Wagner's favor. One way or another, Prigozhin wanted to force Putin to dismiss them.

However, two days before the Wagner plot was to begin, the FSB learned of it. This was critical because mutinies, like coups, benefit from the element of surprise. If Wagner took Shoigu and Gerasimov into custody, Prigozhin would just have to convince everyone else to remain passive and let the situation play out. In contrast, having to track down the pair required the active support of many key players.

The silver lining for Prigozhin was that someone tipped him off that the FSB knew. He then faced a dilemma: give up due to the uphill battle or accelerate the plot. The latter option won out. Wagner's sprint to Rostov-on-Don seemed unaffected, but Shoigu and Gerasimov vanished into thin air. They likely also received word of the plot and made sure to stay away. The key targets of the operation were gone, and Prigozhin lacked a contingency plan.

Still, the rest of the operation was going smoothly. Wagner not only had the strength to take Rostov-on-Don, but they were popular. Both soldiers and civilians voiced support for Prigozhin's actions. Even so, Wagner could not hold onto the city forever. Thus, the convoy departed for Moscow. Somewhere past the halfway point, Prigozhin realized that this was getting out of hand. He did not intend the plot to be a full coup against Putin, but that is what it would become if the convoy entered Moscow. When Putin offered Prigozhin an offramp via Belarusian mediation, he jumped at the chance.

For Western observers, the affair ended in disappointment. This would be no shortcut to the end of the war. Nonetheless, it put Ukraine in a much better position than 24 hours earlier. The cracks in the Russian system were apparent. Wagner's withdrawal from Ukraine limited Russia's ability to threaten further attacks in Donetsk. In fact, Ukraine continued the pressure in Bakhmut, unprepared to give up on the city. Gerasimov disappeared from the public for more than a month. Surovikin, Gerasimov's predecessor as commander of the invasion, appeared to be arrested, and he would not resurface until September. Speculation mounted that he was a secret member of Wagner and had forewarned Prigozhin that the FSB knew of the plot.

Intermission

For a while, it seemed that Wagner went back to business as usual. Prigozhin floated around Moscow and Saint Petersburg, snapping pictures with visiting African dignitaries. Wagner's recruitment centers came back online, looking for mercenaries interested in intercontinental travel. Eventually, reports arose that Prigozhin had indeed reached Belarus. Wagner could continue doing the tasks that the Kremlin appreciated, so long as its soldiers did not get near the capital.

Behind the scenes, Wagner hit some turbulence. For almost a year, Prigozhin lived larger than life, as if playing the role of a character in a grand Russian opera. His rants against the Ministry of Defense defied political norms, but Putin may still have placed some value on keeping Shoigu and Gerasimov in line. The march of justice to Moscow, on the other hand, was a direct challenge to Putin's regime. Even if Prigozhin did not mean to drag Putin into the mix, the optics said otherwise. Prigozhin could no longer be trusted. The Kremlin had to decide whether to follow through on the Belarus-brokered deal or renege.

Prior to the mutiny, the Kremlin had three reasons to keep the group around: plausible deniability, unique military capacity, and avoiding revenge. The plausible deniability aspect was gone. Wagner had become well-known worldwide due to its role in Bakhmut. Given that its forces acted as an extension of the official Russian military, the true nature of Wagner was becoming clear even to casual observers. The mutiny quashed whatever anonymity remained, as the story completely dominated news headlines for the 24 hours it lasted. The true nature of the relationship became official on June 27, when Putin stated that the Kremlin fully financed Wagner all along. Plausible deniability was no longer an argument in favor of Wagner's survival.

Prigozhin further worried that Wagner's irreplaceable military capacity might suddenly find itself very replaceable. That concern dated back to the Ministry of Defense's attempt to integrate all Russian mercenaries into the official armed forces. Wagner's exile to Belarus meant the battle was lost on that front. Still, Wagner had other important holdings, particularly its regime stabilization efforts in Africa. The Kremlin valued keeping those leaders within its sphere of influence and would not want to eliminate Wagner if doing so meant losing those benefits.

As a result, Prigozhin flew to Africa in August. His first stop was to the Central African Republic, with the central message that everything was fine in the world of Wagner. Prigozhin still had ample military assets, even as the Kremlin began confiscating some of Wagner's materiel as a punishment for the mutiny. A group of Sudanese rebels flew in to meet him and pay him gold for Wagner's work on securing a mine. There may have been some phone calls to Niger, where a coup had just taken place. Then Prigozhin headed to neighboring Mali to deliver the same message of continuity.

Whether Wagner actually was unstable remains unclear. Wagner's finances were a black box. It is possible that the mercenary work was directly profitable, as the gift of gold suggests. But it is also possible that the Kremlin subsidized Wagner's operations for the sake of creating some geopolitical instability. Regardless, there was certainly an implicit subsidy in the form of Russian-made materiel—something that was now in jeopardy.

Meanwhile, Russia was not sitting idly by. While Prigozhin went on his African safari, Russian officials also traveled to the continent. The message was flipped: Wagner no longer had the Kremlin's backing. The African affiliates could still enjoy all of the benefits they received from Wagner, but they had to switch to the protection of the Ministry of Defense. That sales pitch must not have been easy given the struggles the Russian military faced in Ukraine. Indeed, it may also help explain why the Kremlin did not immediately eradicate Wagner after the mutiny—the Ministry of Defense simply was not prepared to take over Wagner's African affairs on short notice. But eventually Russia solved that problem.

The last remaining concern was Wagner's retribution. The deal following the mutiny aimed to appease an otherwise angry mob of mercenaries. If they were to ever feel trapped in a corner but still stood a reasonable chance to make a return march on Moscow, they would not hesitate to do so. If an entity could solve that problem, the end of Wagner would follow without issue.

Prigozhin's Final Ballad

On August 23, someone indeed solved the problem. Who exactly did is unclear. The consensus was that the responsible party originated within Russia. But there was no evidence to pin it on someone in particular, whether that be the Ministry of Defense, the FSB, military intelligence, or Putin himself.

The trick came in exploiting a critical flaw in the corporate structure of Wagner. Although Prigozhin became the public face of the group, he was not truly what would be the equivalent of a chief executive officer. Wagner's exact hierarchy was another black box, but he appeared to be more of a chief financial officer and chief marketing officer. That made Prigozhin responsible for the group's accounting and client acquisition. In other words, at the end of the day, he was still a businessman—though his willingness to deploy alongside the rank and file earned him the respect of his comrades.

Instead, the military side of Wagner was under the supervision of Dmitri Utkin, who was best described as the chief operating officer. Utkin was the presumed cofounder of Wagner along with Prigozhin and thus stood at the same level of the corporate ladder. The group also owed its name to his call sign, itself believed to be a reference to German composer Richard Wagner, which in turn might point to connections to neo-Nazis. Utkin was deep into Wagner's affairs and may have commanded the Moscow convoy while Prigozhin stayed back at Rostov-on-Don.

Beyond those two, perhaps the final person in the C-Suite was Valery Chekalov, the functional chief procurement officer. That meant his responsibility was to source and deliver Wagner's materiel to its worldwide interests. Chekalov was likely on a slightly lower tier than Prigozhin or Uktin but still important.

After that was anyone's guess, if any other executives existed at all. Presumably, there was a traditional military chain of command, especially within the locations where Wagner operated. Such a scant organizational chart was likely by design. The more top-level officers there were, the more the group had to pay out. That meant less money staying in the hands of Prigozhin, Utkin, and Chekalov, to whatever extent Chekalov received any of the profits.

However, the tiny C-Suite was also the organization's fatal flaw. Wagner left itself open to a decapitation strike. The minimal solace was that, to succeed, it needed to hit more than just a single individual. If only Prigozhin went down, then Utkin had the ability to mount one final attack on the Kremlin. If only Utkin went down, Prigozhin appointing a new military chief would have solved the issue. Even removing both Prigozhin and Utkin from the equation still left Chekalov to take over. But if Prigozhin, Utkin, and Chekalov all suddenly disappeared, Wagner did not have an obvious future.

In situations like this, the worst outcome for the organization is if its members divide themselves up into factions. The best outcome instead is to have a single successor in charge and for everyone else within the organization to immediately fall in line behind him. But even that would not have guaranteed the continuity of Wagner. Without the C-Suite, the group faced long-term questions about funding and materiel. The Ministry of Defense had answers to those questions and the ability to pay the mercenaries' wages. Defections would come rapidly.

In better institutionalized settings, a clear line of succession deters opponents from attempting such decapitation strikes. For example, if a foreign adversary were to assassinate the U.S. president, the vice president takes over. It is basically impossible to get to a point in the chain of succession where any legal questions arise, and a whole lot of people would have to die before any practical questions would arise either. The same is true within the U.S. military. If the chairman of the joint chiefs of staff or secretary of defense were to be assassinated, the next person would just slot right in. As a result, attempting a random decapitation strike on U.S. officials does not make sense from a strategic standpoint. Such acts would only provoke the United States and result in massive military retaliations.

But Wagner was different. And at around 6 pm on August 23, the mystery perpetrator saw an opening. Prigozhin, Utkin, and Chekalov all took off in a private jet from Moscow, on a short flight to Saint Petersburg. They never made it there. An explosion rocked the plane, causing one of its wings to fall off. The plane stuttered and fell awkwardly to the ground, killing all ten aboard, including Wagner's entire C-Suite.

Why Wagner's leadership congregated on the same flight is a question that will never be answered. In the United States, the president and vice president do not travel on the same plane for this reason. Even if they are headed to the same destination, Air Force One and Air Force Two go separately. It is also common practice with corporations to keep the C-Suite from traveling together—especially the top two individuals. Prigozhin and company certainly knew of the dangers but did it anyway.

In the absence of a clear-cut explanation, there are a few possibilities that might have driven their decision. At a minimum, they must have thought that the Kremlin still viewed Wagner as indispensable despite the Ministry of Defense's encroachments. Beyond that, coordinating security for multiple flights may have been too difficult. They may have also wanted to use the time on the flight to discuss strategy. Perhaps they calculated that no one would be so bold as to stage a plane crash—that if the Kremlin wanted them dead, they would go with the more traditional defenestration or tainted tea routes. Or maybe they were running so short on money they did not have a choice.

Regardless, the powers that be got their wish. Prigozhin paid the ultimate price for his treachery.

Afterword

The name of this book is *How Ukraine Survived*, not *How Ukraine Won.* At this point, Ukraine's survival is almost assured. Russia has shown little ability to hold territory in Western or Central Ukraine and has struggled to maintain its presence in Eastern Ukraine. In all likelihood, Kyiv will stay an independent government.

In contrast, the question of winning the war is up in the air. At the time of writing, Russia still controls a land bridge to Crimea. Ukraine is winding down its first offensive that used Western-trained brigades. I have deliberately left out key moments of the war that occurred well before Prigozhin's assassination, like Russian resistance fighters invading Belgorod, the drone war over Moscow, Russia's reliance on Iran and North Korea for arms (and China's notable lack of help there), and the destruction of the Kakhovka Dam. The reason is that they are a part of the counteroffensive's narrative. Although that narrative is forming, it is not yet complete at the time of writing.

As an early first look, however, the news is not good for Kyiv. Observers anticipated that the counteroffensive would start in the spring. That was inaccurate. The first movements did not begin until June 4, and territorial gains were slow to come by afterward. At least some of the Western tactics taught to Ukrainian soldiers appear to have been misguided, which may have caused the overall plan to sputter. By November 2023, it appeared that Ukraine had run low on artillery, thereby forcing Ukraine to begin culminating its offensive.

Overall, on a tactical level, the offensive seems to have failed. Whether it becomes a strategic success—perhaps by thinning Russian front lines for a future assault once Ukraine has replenished its artillery—remains to be seen. But it has left some Western observers restless, wondering whether a continued attritional approach will ultimately work.

Ukraine cannot win this war on its own. Kyiv has put together a scrappy and resolved fighting force, but the Russian state—despite its many problems with corruption and poorly-managed bureaucracy—is just too large. The difference between survival and victory will be the longevity of Western support. But those chapters are not yet written.

More from William Spaniel

What Caused the Russia-Ukraine War? (And How Will It End?)

Game Theory 101: The Complete Textbook

Game Theory 101: The Rationality of War

Game Theory 101: Bargaining

Bargaining over the Bomb: The Successes and Failures of Nuclear Negotiations

Militant Competition: How Terrorist and Insurgents Advertise with Violence and How They Can Be Stopped

Made in United States
North Haven, CT
04 December 2023

45047235R00124